Christian Voices in Unitarian Universalism

CHRISTIAN VOICES IN UNITARIAN UNIVERSALISM

CONTEMPORARY ESSAYS

Edited by Kathleen Rolenz

SKINNER HOUSE BOOKS
BOSTON

Copyright © 2006 by the Unitarian Universalist Association of Congregations. Published by Skinner House Books, an imprint of the Unitarian Universalist Association of Congregations, a liberal religious organization with more than 1,000 congregations in the U.S. and Canada, 25 Beacon St., Boston, MA 02108-2800.

Cover design by Kathryn Sky-Peck
Text design by Suzanne Morgan

Printed in the United States

ISBN 1-55896-506-8
978-1-55896-506-5

09 08 07 06
5 4 3 2 1

Library of Congress Cataloging-in-Publication Data

Christian voices in Unitarian Universalism : contemporary essays / edited by Kathleen Rolenz.
    p. cm.
 ISBN-13: 978-1-55896-506-5 (pbk. : alk. paper)
 ISBN-10: 1-55896-506-8 (pbk. : alk. paper) 1. Christian biography—United States. 2. Unitarian Universalists—Biography. I. Rolenz, Kathleen.

BX9867.C47 2006
289.1'32—dc22   2006007320

"In God's House There Are Many Rooms" is adapted from portions of *Finding Your Religion: When the Faith You Grew Up With Has Lost Its Meaning* by Scotty McLennan, 2001.

Contents

Foreword by Carl Scovel — vii

Introduction — ix

A Bible-Thumping, Trinitarian, Charismatic,
Born-Again Jesus Freak — 1
   Rachel Nguyen

Walking the Walk — 9
   Anita Farber-Robertson

God Is Not Through with Me Yet — 15
   Terry Mark Burke

A Pathway Home — 25
   Robert Fabre

The Pilgrimage of a Catholic UU — 29
   Peter Huff

Learning to Love the Questions — 45
   Cricket Potter

Pain, Psalm, Prayer and a Promise *Ron Robinson*	49
3-D Jesus *Kathleen Rolenz*	61
A Mad Mix of Dedicated People *John Simcox*	67
The Advocate *Carol Stamatakis*	71
Why I Left Unitarian Universalism *Kay Achar*	85
An Old Friend *Erik Walker Wikstrom*	91
I Am Convicted *Victoria Weinstein*	99
To Keep One's Soul *Marjorie Bowens-Wheatley*	109
In God's House There Are Many Rooms *Scotty McLennan*	117
A New Spirit	123
For Further Reading	129

Foreword

The essays in this book testify to something considered unlikely, if not impossible, forty years ago: Unitarian Universalists reclaiming the power of Christianity. These women and men are typical of Unitarian Universalism in that their authors arrive at their liberal Christian faith by several different paths. Their spiritual guides include a Bedouin, an AME preacher, a monk, atheist parents, an angry hometown pastor, an Anglican priest, and a church ladies' guild. Some of the crucial influences along the way are as traditional as the Bible or a traumatic event but others are more surprising—performances of *Jesus Christ Superstar* and the Bernstein mass or watching a client testify in court.

This collection shows the continuing relevance and vitality of our Christian roots in Unitarian Universalism and how the Christian faith can transform and intellectually excite thoughtful seekers. Personal stories are a testament to the uniqueness of each individual—we are all moved and transformed in different ways. These witnesses point toward a Jesus who is not just human but humane, not just in touch with God but in touch with them. This Jesus is relational, robust, and real. Victoria Weinstein writes, "Jesus Christ is to me the freedom that laughs uproariously at the things of this world, while loving me dearly for being human enough to lust after them." For Anita Farber-Robertson, Jesus is primarily an advocate: "I wanted a Jesus who could teach me how to hate the sin and not the sinner, how to fight the good fight, even when it seemed unwinnable." No two people relate to Jesus or God in exactly the same way.

Spiritual longings and the quests we undertake to fulfill them are personal and distinctive. What all of these writers have in common is love for and faith in a holy man who lived thousands of years ago and the determination to walk in his path.

Carl Scovel

Introduction

"Who do men say that I am?" asked Jesus of his disciple Peter. It's a question that continues to haunt Unitarian Universalists to this day. For Christian Unitarian Universalists, it is the task and focus of their faith—to continue to uncover the mystery behind the message of Jesus. For non-Christian UUs, Jesus continues to draw crowds. When scholars like John Dominic Crossan or Marcus Borg speak at the local community college or at General Assembly, the workshops are standing-room only. When ministers or lay leaders offer classes on the Bible or on Jesus, they report high attendance. Members of many UU congregations are becoming more comfortable with Jesus as an object of study—although not as an inspiration for worship. At the same time, a growing number of Unitarian Universalists are "coming out" of their self-imposed closets to name what Jesus means to them. A growing number of seminarians are comfortable with God language, Bible study, and spiritual direction. Furthermore, there have always been Christian Unitarian Universalists who have kept the work and spirit of Jesus alive in this movement.

The idea for this book was generated from a panel discussion sponsored by the Unitarian Universalist Christian Fellowship, entitled "Jesus for the Twenty-First Century," at General Assembly in Long Beach, California. Four panelists were asked to respond to Erik Wikstrom's book, *Teacher, Guide, Companion: Rediscovering Jesus in a Secular World.* As one of the respondents, I wondered what approach I should take. Should I offer a scholarly opinion about Wikstrom's research? Should I research and offer my opinion about the latest findings from the Jesus Seminar? Perhaps I should provide facts and figures about Jesus' life? In the end, I decided against all of these. I thought a simple telling of my story, of how I came to call myself a Christian Unitarian Universalist, would be sufficient. I wanted my listeners to know how much Jesus means to me—and of the journey that led me to that place. After the panel discussion, several people approached me and wanted to talk about *their* stories—of how Jesus had always been in their lives and of how they had to make room for him as Unitarian Universalists. I heard stories about their long and arduous journeys toward Jesus. I heard about the difficulties of holding on to their Unitarian Universalist identities. I was humbled to note that many UUs have quietly maintained their membership in the Unitarian Universalist Christian movement for many years. I spoke with people who came to the workshop out of an intellectual curiosity about Jesus and found themselves strangely moved by the personal testimonies of the panelists.

I wanted to hear more stories, from both clergy and laity alike, as to who Jesus is for Unitarian Universalists today. Does he have increasing importance as a religious figure not only for discussion groups but also as the object of worship? Can Jesus' message speak across the millennia to contemporary non-Christian Unitarian Universalists? What might the future hold for twenty-first–century Christian Unitarian Universalists? These are but a few of the questions that will be raised and discussed in this collection of essays.

Kathleen Rolenz

A Bible-Thumping, Trinitarian, Charismatic, Born-Again Jesus Freak

RACHEL NGUYEN

I have been slain by the Spirit, I have conversations with God while driving on the highway, and I would take up snake handling if I had something other than garter snakes to practice on. I am full-blown in love with God and have completely accepted that Jesus *really is* my personal savior. And I am a lifelong Unitarian Universalist.

I am *not* an evangelist. I have not come to believe that Jesus must be your personal savior. I don't even necessarily believe that anyone else needs saving. But *I* do. I know that I have spent too much of my life feeling fair to middling about the world and my place in it. I know I dreamed that someday I would actually feel lighthearted and joyous. That I would live a life of connection to God and Spirit and to everyone in the world. And I came to believe that the only way to do that was to develop a better relationship with

God. Which is how Jesus came into the picture. Jesus, as you may recall, had a positively amazing relationship with God. Whether you believe that he was the Word incarnate or just a really special guy, you have to admit that he had the God thing down. He performed all kinds of miracles and then went off to pray. He spent forty days in the desert wrangling the devil and came out in time to turn water into wine at a wedding. He loved his enemies to the point of saving the lives of their children. He cured the blind, the deaf, and the mentally ill. He spent time with his daddy in prayer. He knew that we all have the potential to create the Kingdom of God right here and now.

I haven't always been a Christian. My mother, a third-generation atheist and a lapsed, garden-variety Protestant, raised me as an unchurched UU. The only discussions we ever had about religion involved her summer Bible camp experiences, which included a lot of pranks and practical jokes, buckets of ice water, and Saran Wrap on toilet seats. Religion, per se, was not on our radar screen.

I didn't start to realize I needed to work on a better relationship with God until I was an adult. I came to understand that if left to my own devices I drifted toward misery and unhappiness just as surely as a leaf drifts downstream. I could try to will myself toward the light but, inevitably, would come up against my own tendency toward despair.

My relationship with God began in earnest about fifteen years ago. My mom was diagnosed with a brain tumor. She had surgery to remove the growth, and it was successful. During her recovery, though, some strange things started to happen. She began to have spiritual visions and experiences.

For example, my mother had a dinner party for some women friends. After a light meal of soup and bread, we sat around the dining room table and joined hands in prayer. My mother led the prayer, asking God to join us in the room, for the Holy Spirit to become present. Suddenly, the five of us were overwhelmed by a distinct energy force in the center of the table. The energy actually had an edge to it that we could feel when we lifted our hands. We all had our eyes closed but were holding our hands up to feel this spirit, this energy. While sitting there, I had a vision. I saw myself in the middle of a cloud of mist. I saw that this cloud encompassed every other living being in the universe, and I became aware that the cloud that encompassed all of us was, in fact, God. I suddenly understood that psychic phenomenon was simply crossing the cloud of mist, that we really were all part of the same whole. I began to laugh, and even cry a little bit. It was as if I were recognizing a primal truth and I couldn't believe that something so simple had escaped me for so long. When we all finally opened our eyes we were all crying and all holding our hands up like worshipers do in paintings of the saints or the Madonna, in the way priests invoke the Holy Spirit during the Eucharist.

This unexpected, deep awareness of God had a huge impact on me, but at the time I didn't have a sense of what to do with it. After all, I didn't identify myself as a Christian. So for years I was unchurched and self-taught, delving into tarot and Kabbalah and other occult systems that attempted to explain the nature of the Divine.

So where did the Christian thing come in?

Several years after my "experience" I began to long for more depth in my relationship with God. I felt that something was missing. While I believed that we were all connected through God, it was hard to actually put that belief into practice with the guy who just cut me off on the highway. I was looking for some kind of spiritual practice that would help me live my faith on a daily basis.

I began to have Jesus envy. I would listen longingly to the relationships that friends of mine had with Jesus and see how he was such a big presence in their lives, but I just couldn't seem to get over the issues of theology and dogma. I didn't believe in original sin, for example, so how could I buy the idea that Jesus died for my sins? And the mainline church's stance on things like tarot reading and homosexuality just didn't sit right with me, given my personal belief in a loving God.

When I found the UU church three years ago, I met with my new minister, Steve Landale, and one of my very first questions was "Can a UU be a Christian?" His answer was honest. "It can be a challenge," he said. My next question was "What is the nature of sin?" This at our first meeting. Poor Steve.

He handed me a book by Marcus Borg, called *Meeting Jesus Again for the First Time.* For me this book was revolutionary because its premise is that one didn't have to *believe* in any particular dogma in order to be a Christian; one simply has to *want* to be in relationship with God, something that Jesus was amazing at. Borg goes on to say that Christianity doesn't have to be a religion about Jesus, but is, in fact, the religion of what Jesus was always pointing toward, the Divine. This was a huge shift in perspective.

I met with Steve again a few months later, and as we were talking I began to think about getting baptized. I didn't mention my idea to Steve right away but thought about it for several months. Frankly, I wasn't even sure he would do it. When I finally asked him, I explained that I wanted to have a ritual baptism, one that would signify giving my life over to God. It wouldn't be a Christian thing, I said, more of a God thing. For the whole summer before the baptism, I scouted locations, dragging my husband, Nguyen, and my two kids to rivers and ponds all over Massachusetts and Rhode Island. Finally, I found the place—a little pond on the Connecticut border with a waterfall and stream running off it. The location was beautiful.

On the morning of the baptism, it was one of those shockingly clear and cool September days. There were no clouds in the sky. We drove to the pond together—my mom, Nguyen, Steve, and I. The kids were in school. When we got to the pond there were a couple of fishermen on the opposite bank. It was absolutely calm and quiet. We stood in a circle on the beach and held hands and said our prayers and asked God to bless this event. My mother read a piece by Thomas Merton. Then Steve and I walked into the water. When we got about waist high, I read my vows and Steve lowered me into the water backwards. My eyes were closed, but I remember seeing everything. The image of the water closing over me. The whiteness of Steve's robes. His hands pulling me back up too soon. I went down a second time because I wanted to relish the feeling of being suspended in the water, which felt so warm to me, even on a chilly September morning. Later, back on the beach, I couldn't stop laughing.

I didn't tell my atheist dad about the baptism for several days. I think I was concerned that he would feel compelled to joke about it, and I wasn't ready to hear that just yet. When I finally told him, I made a big point of saying that the baptism wasn't a Christian thing, it was a God thing. He pointedly commented, "Oh, it was a Christian thing." I hung up the phone, surprised.

Three days later, I sensed Jesus sitting on my doorstep. I began to believe that my act of surrender to God might involve Jesus, too. I realized that maybe God wanted me to look to Jesus as a way of deepening my relationship with him. I also realized that if I didn't open the door, Jesus was never going leave me alone. So I sat in my living room one morning and invited Jesus into my heart.

The years since my baptism have been the most amazing of my life. Tough ones, yes. Loss and death in the midst of unparalleled joy and discovery. Being a Christian is the best thing in my life, and lots of hard work. I find that I need daily contact with God in order to be able to walk this path. I spend forty minutes a day in prayerful meditation. I read my Bible daily. On occasion I go to a local Anglican church, St. Stephen's, to take communion, and I meet with an Anglican priest once a month for spiritual counseling. Steve and I get together regularly to discuss the effects of the baptism and the challenge of being a Christian UU. The irony is, of course, that I was only able to become a Christian *because* I was a UU. I am not sure I would have been able to get past the issues of dogma and theology in a traditional Christian church. It's even more ironic that after I got baptized, all the rational reservations I had about Christianity ceased to be relevant. Now I understand that some deep transformation is occurring within me, and it isn't necessarily a rational thing. What I know is that finally, for the first time in my life, I am genuinely filled with joy.

I am grateful to my Unitarian Universalist church, Bell Street Chapel, in Providence, Rhode Island, for giving me a safe place to explore my faith. Yes, there are times when I long to be in community with other Christians, and there may come a day when that longing draws me to leave the UU faith, but for me, being a Christian is fundamentally about learning to live as though God dwells within all of us. The Unitarian Universalist Church, with its emphasis on social action and diversity of faith, is a joyful place for me to practice this most sacred calling.

―◦―

RACHEL H. NGUYEN *is an active member of the Religious Society of Bell Street Chapel in Providence, Rhode Island. She is a natural childbirth educator, professional tarot reader, and teacher.*

Walking the Walk

ANITA FARBER-ROBERTSON

I was born with twin longings: the longing for God and the longing for justice. As a child I had clear words for the second and an inarticulate hungering for the first. This was natural. My parents had met at a Young People's Socialist Party picnic. I grew up in a home that bristled with a fierce passion for justice and a deep distrust of religion. My father had witnessed the church's shameful inability to stand up to the Nazis. He eventually left Germany on the last boat for the United States before Germany marched on Poland. My mother had experienced the devaluing of women in her New York Orthodox Jewish home, where she had to fight for the right to higher education. My parents loved justice, and they saw organized religion as one of its impediments.

I, on the other hand, loved God. I didn't know what that meant exactly, but I knew I did, and I had a sense of the benevolent presence of one who held and was the universe, and who held me in love. I loved that God who had given me life and who had infused in me the love of others, which in turn fed my thirst for justice. But I couldn't put all of that together then. They seemed distinctly separate. I could speak about my love for justice openly, explore it with my parents, take risks to satisfy it without inviting parental displeasure. But I needed to keep my love for God secret from my parents. They alternately discounted or excoriated a supreme being who comforted the comfortable and was used by the affluent to justify the oppression of the lower classes.

Although my Lutheran grandmother had once taken me to church and my Jewish grandmother had once taken me to synagogue, those were visits without context that gave me no understanding of organized religion. My only positive experience of religion came from the Passover seder we held each year. The seder text had been written by a humanist friend of the family and was a powerful retelling of a story of liberation, of a people who believed that their God loved justice. The last glass of wine each year was lifted to "the liberation of all people everywhere." I loved the story, and I loved the God of liberation. I still do.

The civil rights movement gripped this country and me when I was in high school. I marched, I sang, I raised money, I worked for candidates, I organized concerts and demonstrations, I found the black church. I did not understand the theology of the black church, and I knew little about Christianity. But I was learning gospel hymns about a God who loved freedom and who walked with the oppressed when they marched and when they suffered. Jesus knew these people, and in him they had a friend in the struggle. My mind could not make sense of this, but my heart could. I sang those spirituals with an aching empathy that captured what I had no words to say.

The peace movement came—more white, more secular. It was passionate but not soulful. Gone were the deep religious metaphors and undertones. I worked for peace, and I put my spiritual questions aside. I had no one to share them with.

After I got married and moved away from New York City, I began to think again about religious questions, about my need to find a way to speak with this God who hovered, and sometimes alighted, in my life. I knew I wanted community, a way to make this new house truly my home. I went to liberal Protestant churches for which Judaism was merely the preamble to Christianity, not a fully formed spirituality of its own. I joined a liberal Reform Jewish congregation, where people were nice enough but offered no place to talk about who Jesus was. So, I continued working with secular causes and organizations to make my own community of meaning. But then one day I was invited to the Unitarian Universalist Fellowship. I was both delighted and chagrined to find that I knew about a third of the people sitting in the congregation. I was delighted to find friends, but disappointed that they had never told me about this church where you could go to be encouraged and recharge your batteries. I was a humanist, as were they. Humanism was the only language I knew—and the fellowship was about to give me a place to begin exploring my own faith.

The exploration was compelling, leading me to my decision to attend an interdenominational seminary so I could have the broadest conversations possible as I studied for the ministry. I chose Andover Newton. There I was tried and pushed and tested as a religious humanist becoming a theist, but I was still somewhat distrustful of and puzzled by Christianity. Slowly, I began to learn its language, which was important if I was going to participate meaningfully in an interfaith world.

I loved my God of justice. I love that God still. And that God rested on my shoulder, so it seemed, as I took up a parish ministry. Prayer became a part of my life, alone and in groups of colleagues. Jesus was a shadowy figure. Occasionally I might pull the curtain and expose him when he was pedagogically useful, but then I'd tidy up and put him safely away.

My parents had given up the struggle for justice. They'd gotten tired, burned out. When I took up their work in high school, they'd been happy to give it over to me. I knew others who had worked hard in their younger years and become cynical and pessimistic. I did not want that to happen to me.

Over my years of interfaith community organizing I came to know Christians of many different types. Working in Lynn, Massachusetts, as part of the Essex County Community Organization, something extraordinary and transforming happened to me. I worked with African-American pastors of churches that struggled to pay their heating bills, who saw beloved church leaders crushed by their children's drug habits, who saw neighbors in the throes of grief when a child was killed in a shooting, who saw communities gather around families struck by tragedy, who were generous beyond comprehension, and who worked tirelessly for justice. And they were kind. They were compassionate. They did not lose their empathy over time, or their sensitivity. They looked at these people Jesus loved and loved them too. Their Jesus gave them the strength to fight, the courage to love, and hearts that do not give up on anyone. I saw privileged white pastors remain seated at the table as they listened to difficult truths because of Jesus, and because those who spoke represented "the least of these" and were therefore themselves the Christ. People worked hard, not only in the name and spirit of Jesus, but because Jesus companioned and sustained them, loved them in the midst of rage and frustration, and allowed them to love their enemies.

I wanted that Jesus in my life. I wanted a Jesus who could teach me how to hate the sin and not the sinner, how to fight the good fight even when it seemed unwinnable. I wanted that Jesus who loved everyone, regardless of his or her faults or deficiencies. I wanted that Jesus who would love *me*.

It was not, however, going to be enough to want Jesus in my life. I was going to have to claim him, and let him claim me. I was going to have to say, "Yes, this is my path.

You are my guide, my teacher, and my savior, for without you my soul would get brittle, my mouth grow bitter, my heart hard."

My life has changed since I made that decision for Jesus, for God, for myself. It has gotten more difficult in many ways. I am an anomaly in my family and with my colleagues. But I now have a God who is a presence, not just a theory. I have a God who understands my human life and cares so much about it that he is willing to slip into human form, wrap the skin of finitude, life and death, and even gender around himself, and walk the humbling walk of humankind.

This is a God I can love with all my heart, all my soul, all my mind, and all my strength. And this God, who walks with me in Jesus, and who sings with me in the spirit, keeps me keeping on, in the journey toward wholeness, toward justice, toward love.

―◦―

ANITA FARBER-ROBERTSON *has been a Unitarian Universalist parish minister for nearly twenty-five years. She also enjoys full ministerial standing with the American Baptist Churches. She serves as the interim minister at the Walpole Unitarian Church in New Hampshire and does church development consulting with a United Church of Christ congregation in Maine. Dr. Farber-Robertson is most recently the author of* Learning While Leading: Increasing Your Effectiveness in Ministry.

GOD IS NOT THROUGH WITH ME YET

TERRY MARK BURKE

I was born in Flint, Michigan, to parents in a "mixed" Catholic-Protestant marriage. Their experience with religion had been so disagreeable when they got married that they joined the ranks of the unchurched. They raised my brother Tim and me with a basic, if vague, belief in God and strong ethical values. Growing up, my closest friend, Kirby, and I visited various churches together. Kirby later converted to Catholicism and became a Benedictine monk for twelve years. I majored in English literature in college and was required to take a course on the King James Version of the Bible. It was the first time I had ever read the Bible, and I was intrigued. I also discovered John Donne's poem "Good Friday, 1613, Riding Westward" on Good Friday, 1973, and wondered if I, too, was traveling away from God.

Following the crowd, I applied to law school, but then decided to take my summer savings and travel in Europe instead. After visiting churches in Chartres, Assisi, Sienna, and Venice, I landed in Paris. I supported myself working illegally: babysitting, teaching English, opening scallops, and cleaning office buildings.

My cleaning coworkers were Nigerian students who lived in horrendous conditions, five students to a small "maid's room." One of the Nigerian students had a psychological breakdown when I was working with him. He kept saying to the French woman who was our supervisor, "I'll kill you and I'll kill myself!" She didn't understand English, but we finally got him to calm down and go home. Brought face-to-face with suffering and evil, I began to think about going into the ministry.

I returned to the States, worked at a used bookstore, and audited classes in classical Greek at Harvard. At the bookstore I met a friendly divinity student, and our conversations got me interested in applying to the master's in theological studies program at Harvard Divinity School. I studied early and Byzantine church history with the great church historian George Williams, a Unitarian Universalist, who once brought into class the icons that he'd been given by Ecumenical Patriarch Athenagoras.

I supported myself with a staff job at a residence for deinstitutionalized mental patients. Although I kept trying to explain to the residents that I was in an academic program at divinity school, it didn't seem to make any difference. They continued to place me in the role of their chaplain, and eventually I grew into it. I found that ministering to others was much more meaningful to me than the academic study of religion.

I switched to the ministerial master's of divinity program and became affiliated with the Unitarian Universalist Association as a divinity student. (I had attended a Unitarian church in Flint when I was in high school. My friends in the antiwar movement had gone there.) Around this same time a close friend asked me to pray for her. This was something new for me, not a childish "Now I lay me down to sleep . . . ." Out of respect for my friend I complied, and found that prayer was important to me.

As part of my ministerial training I did field education work at the Charles Street AME (African Methodist Episcopal) Church in Roxbury, Massachusetts. The pastor, Donald Luster, asked me, "Now, some Unitarian Universalists are Christians, and some think Jesus was just a great prophet and teacher. Who is Jesus Christ for you?" I admitted I wasn't sure who Jesus was to me, but I thought he might be more than a prophet and teacher. Rev. Luster replied, "I think that the Lord has work for us."

Soon after that I moved into the vacant parsonage of the Roxbury Presbyterian Church with my friend and fellow seminarian Chris Hedges. As a pastor, I learned to pray extemporaneously, trusting in the spirit and a few images I'd think up while walking to church. I was deeply moved by the congregants, who reached out to me as a white person in an all-black church; these were people who in their everyday lives "walked the streets with Jesus."

One Wednesday I was asked to be the preacher at the midweek evening service at Charles Street AME. My fellow seminarians were leading the service, and the "Mothers of the Church," respected churchwomen who wore white deaconess outfits, told me to wait in the vestry and prepare myself until the time to preach. During the prayers, I heard one of the Mothers praying for me—for my preaching of God's word and for my life in Christ. It seemed to me at that moment that if these good people who tried to live a life in Christ trusted and believed in me, I would try to live a life in Christ, too.

I tried to understand what my new identity as a UU Christian meant for me. Following Professor James Luther Adams's example, I began to meet with a Catholic nun at the Center for Religious Development in Cambridge for spiritual direction. "Can you imagine that God might be personal?" was the question she asked in my intake interview. I also started talking with Rev. Carl Scovel of King's Chapel, a UU Christian congregation, about baptism. Attending a UU conference in Berkeley, California, I went with friends one night to see a film based on Flannery O'Connor's story *Wise Blood*. Afterward I got lost trying to find my way back to the graduate housing. It was cold and drizzling rain. "Hell is like this," I thought, and when I returned to Boston I joined the UU Christian Fellowship.

I was baptized at King's Chapel on All Saints' Day, 1981. A friend had just returned from her honeymoon in the Holy Land, and she gave me some water from the Jordan

River for my baptism. It burned when it was placed upon my forehead.

My baptism remains central to my religious self-understanding. As part of the confession of faith that Carl Scovel had me write, I said, "I believe that God seeks a loving, dialogical relationship with humanity, and that the life, death, and resurrection of Jesus Christ calls us to reflect that sacrificial love in our lives. The cross and the faithful community proclaim that it is more important to love than to survive and that love is stronger than death."

As I was finishing my studies at seminary I was also receiving training in spiritual direction from the Jesuits at the Campion Center in Weston, Massachusetts. With their help, I prayerfully decided to go ahead with my ordination at the Universalist Church of New York City, where I had served as an intern. I was ordained to the Ministry of Word and Sacrament in the churches and fellowships of the Unitarian Universalist Association on April 25, 1982, the Feast of St. Mark.

In the course of finding a calligrapher for my ordination announcement, I met and fell in love with Ellen McGuire. Ellen and I were married six months later. In 1983 I started working as a UU urban extension minister, a denominational appointee to a tiny congregation of primarily elderly people in the Jamaica Plain neighborhood of Boston. Ellen was already the organist and clerk of the church. When I feared that this might be a conflict of interest, a UU official said, "Oh no, that'll give you a wonderful entrée with the elderly parishioners." The church had a strong liturgical tradition with an emphasis on music and prayer and was located in a diverse urban neighborhood. The congregation's bond of fellowship is the Ames Covenant: "In the love of truth, and in the spirit of Jesus, we unite for the worship of God, and the service of humanity."

I began a spiritual direction program with Carl Scovel, who has remained my friend and mentor. In 1984, I was hospitalized for two weeks with a high fever, which was finally diagnosed as a complication of appendicitis. After I recovered, I visited my former roommate, Chris Hedges, now a journalist in El Salvador. I traveled around the countryside with Chris and met people like Lutheran Bishop Medardo Gomez, who had been tortured for his work with the poor. I also saw the chapel where Archbishop Oscar Romero was murdered while celebrating the Eucharist.

The Jamaica Plain congregation grew, with our ministry emphasizing spiritual growth and social justice. Ellen and I endured five miscarriages. During this time, a UU colleague sent me a postcard of the Vladimir Mother of God icon, which, quite uncharacteristically, I put up in our front hallway. I regard the later birth of our older daughter, after a very difficult pregnancy and delivery, as a special gift from Mary. We now have three wonderful children.

On Easter Sunday in 1990 I rose at five in the morning for the early worship service in our parish graveyard. Glancing at the previous day's mail, I noticed a workshop on Eastern Orthodox iconography. Although I'd had little contact with icons or any experience studying art, I felt called to this work. Writing about the icon of the Archangel Michael brought me into contact with the mystical traditions of the Eastern Church, in which icons are seen as windows that help us connect to spiritual reality.

My appreciation of that mystical tradition has deepened as a result of my two sabbaticals in 1993 and 2001. During the first, I studied the meaning of the dark brown skin tones in traditional Russian icons and what our color-obsessed society could learn from such icons. I was blessed to study with Ksenia Pokrovsky, a Russian iconographer and a recent immigrant to the Boston area.

Ksenia and her husband, Lev, had been congregants of Father Alexander Menn, who was murdered (probably by the KGB). Although both Lev and Ksenia are scientists, Father Menn convinced Ksenia thirty years ago that she needed to revive traditional practices of iconography. The Pokrovskys share their teacher's ecumenical approach and are a powerful model for me of scientists and intellectuals of faith.

Later in that sabbatical, my childhood friend Kirby (who'd left the Benedictines and was now Eastern Orthodox) invited me to accompany him on a visit to the New Skete monastery in Cambridge, New York. This was the first time I had attended an Eastern liturgy, which attempts to convey the beauty and mystical presence of the Kingdom of God. The head of the monastery, Father Lawrence, gave me copies of their liturgical books. As a result of his generosity, I incorporated some of this spiritual practice into my prayer life.

During my second sabbatical, in 2001, I had a grant from the Lilly Endowment to study how women are portrayed in traditional iconography. The grant included travel for my family, and my son Willis and I visited museums, churches, and monasteries in Greece and climbed the "Holy Mountain," Mount Athos, in "Mary's garden." On a month-long trip by myself, I traveled to Russia, where I was deeply moved by the "Troitsky Sobor" or Trinity Cathedral at the monastery complex in Zagorsk. This had been the original home of the Andrei Rublev icon of the Trinity, which shows the three angels who appear to Abraham and Sarah in Genesis 18; the three are addressed in the text in the singular as "Lord." When my daughter Amelia was little, she saw a copy of this icon and asked me what it was. I tried to explain that the Trinity icon showed God as a loving community. Pointing to the central figure, she said, "*that* one is Jesus." And she was right.

My father, Jack Burke, had died on the feast of Saint Ksenia, and I visited her tomb in St. Petersburg. Ksenia was an eighteenth-century aristocrat who gave up her wealth to live as a homeless "holy fool," helping poor families. After locating my father's aunt in Bialystok, I flew to Istanbul, the "New Rome," where I had the opportunity to meet Ecumenical Patriarch Bartholomew. I gave the patriarch a quilted coin purse that Ellen had made; instead of a good luck coin, I'd placed a cross inside. Bartholomew opened the purse, took out the cross, and immediately kissed it.

Also on this journey, I saw the wonderful icons of Saint

Catherine's Monastery at Mount Sinai. Since Saint Catherine is a patron of scholars, the monastery's library has one of the finest collections of manuscripts in the world. I climbed the "steps of repentance" up Mount Sinai with my Bedouin guide, Jose. On top of Mount Sinai, a friend of Jose's gave us bread and a delicious lentil dish. "What do I owe you for this great meal?" I asked afterward. "Nothing," the man replied, "this is Bedouin hospitality."

I am a Unitarian Universalist Christian for two reasons. I feel gratitude to a tradition that was willing to risk ordaining a raw young man into spiritual leadership. I also feel called to serve the "living icons" who are members of our Jamaica Plain church community, thankful to share the pains and joys of human life. I hope that, in the words of a gospel hymn, "God is not through with me yet."

―◦―

TERRY MARK BURKE *is a Unitarian Universalist minister and serves the First Church in Jamaica Plain, Massachusetts. He lives in the Roslindale neighborhood of Boston.*

A Pathway Home

ROBERT FABRE

The theme of a General Assembly I attended several years ago in Phoenix, Arizona, was interfaith cooperation. It might well have been called *intrafaith* cooperation. Everywhere I went, I met people who called themselves UU Christians, UU Buddhists, UU humanists, UU pagans, or UU Jews, but not many people who called themselves simply Unitarian Universalist. Why not?

I think that particular term is simply not meaningful enough. I personally belong to a faith community that defines itself as both Unitarian Universalist *and* Christian. My Christian identity is of vital importance to me. It informs me of who I am and what I believe in. By the same token, I am also a Unitarian Universalist because I believe that revelation is not sealed. I choose to associate with people who are also searching for answers in other faith communities. The question this raises is, how can I be both? How can I be both a Christian and belong to a larger movement that is largely non-Christian? I don't have a clear answer, but I do know that it's possible. I am 100 percent Christian, 100 percent identified with the larger Christian church, part of the body of Christ. I am also 100 percent Unitarian Universalist, 100 percent identified with both my local church and with the larger UU movement. Is this impossible, an inherent contradiction? Yes, absolutely. But is it true? Yes.

My path has been a long one. I left the Presbyterian Church at an early age when I could no longer believe or understand what it was trying to teach me. The idea of the trinity, for example, of "three persons in one Godhead," was, in my mind, at best a misguided concept, at worst nonsense. I stayed away from institutional religion until I was close to thirty years old, when I found myself in a new town with a new set of needs and desires. I wanted to find a spiritual community that I could call home. I found that community in the UU church.

Being in a liberal religious community gave me the freedom to search for answers, unbound by an expected creed or set of beliefs. And I found, to my amazement, that the answer for me was Christianity. But it was a new type of Christianity. My Christianity does not dwell so much on the divinity of Jesus as it does on who he was as a man and the message he preached. Jesus offered a radical challenge that was both impossible to meet and impossible to ignore. He preached that "God is love," that love is so overpowering a force, so overwhelming a demand, that we are called even to love our enemies and, through that process, turn them into our friends. He taught us that suffering, even death, is not the final answer; God is the final answer. This is the message that Jesus proclaimed, that he lived and died for, that he invites us to live and die for.

So Unitarian Universalism was, for me, the pathway back to Christianity. No doubt I wouldn't be where I am today, wouldn't be the person I am today, without it. Ironically, the longer I've been associated with this liberal religious community, the more conservative I've become on a personal level. So now I can say, I believe that Jesus was the son of God (not God but the son of God); I believe in the resurrection (not the resuscitation of a dead body but the resurrection); and I believe that I am saved by grace (not because I accept Jesus as my personal savior but because, despite my confusion and my unbelief, despite my shortcomings and mistakes, in a mysterious way, beyond my comprehension and explanation, God accepts me).

Most UUs have different spiritual paths—humanist, pagan, Jewish, agnostic, atheist. But we've all found a home in this religious movement. In the end, we are all on the same journey—the journey to ultimate meaning.

Unitarian Universalism is at a crucial stage. We are pushing the limits of our boundaries. On the one hand, Unitarian Universalism is not a religion where you can believe anything you want. That is chaos, not community. On the other hand, in a religious movement that does not have a creed, the limits of our tolerance—our acceptance—

are exceedingly broad. What we have to do is stop pretending we're all alike, stop pretending that there are certain orthodoxies that we all believe (for example, there is a God, or there is no God), and start accepting the real differences among us. A Buddhist does not believe the same things that a Christian believes. A Christian does not believe the same things that a humanist believes. What holds us together at the edges, as we are on the verge of flying apart, is the idea, the reality, of the beloved community. As Francis David said, "We don't have to think alike to love alike." Or as Jesus put it, "In my father's house, there are many rooms."

As members of this community, let us be together, let us reason together, let us love together, let us be a model for the larger world, then let us go out into this larger world and witness our faith.

ROBERT FABRE *is an attorney-editor for a legal publisher. He attends the Unitarian Universalist Church of Akron, Ohio.*

The Pilgrimage
of a Catholic UU

PETER HUFF

Back when I was a teenager and a Southern Baptist, my undisciplined efforts at honest evening prayer would occasionally concentrate on a specific question arising from my first serious experiments in Christology, the theological study of Jesus' deeds and teachings. I was a theologically precocious adolescent, having read Saint Augustine's *On Christian Doctrine* in eighth grade (and boasted about it in my high school newspaper). My bedtime prayer, however, was as simple and unpretentious as it was earnest. "Tell me who you are," I whispered into the dark. I knew I was exploring uncharted spiritual territory—what today I would call the liminal space between conventional belief and outright unbelief. But I also realized that I had to face what was becoming an increasingly important personal issue. My prayer, addressed to Jesus, was a sincere plea for insight into the true identity of the Christ who had dominated and even haunted my childhood spirituality but who had somehow recently slipped into a realm clouded by confusion.

Admittedly more demand than request, my prayer was a surprisingly reverent way of confessing to myself, and whatever other power might have access to my thoughts at the time, that Jesus Christ had clearly taken on the status of a problem. What strikes me now is not so much the uncertainty communicated by my youthful prayer but its undisguised note of intellectual curiosity. Yes, I had a problem on my hands. But somehow I instinctively recognized that the problem of Jesus could be a delicious sort of problem—the kind that stirs the imagination of a scientist or a detective. In my solitary passage from unexamined belief to active doubt, I began to discover just how satisfying open-ended theological investigation could be.

My adventures in Christology began in the age of *Jesus Christ Superstar*, *Godspell*, and Zeffirelli's *Jesus of Nazareth*. Countercultural images of Jesus challenged the icons of the academy and popular religion, and critics saw the upstart Christs as dangerous threats to conventional orthodoxy and mainstream values. I was largely unaware of the wide variety of portraits of Jesus in the historic Christian intellectual tradition, but I quickly realized that the new Christs crossing my path could never be accommodated in the evangelical folk piety of my suburban family or the seemingly innocuous Sunday School literature of my culturally captive Protestant denomination. To my untrained theological mind, these bold and imaginative Christologies presented a composite Jesus who was far more mystical, introspective, brooding—and human—than any Jesus I had encountered before. The new Christ inspired me to submit everything I had previously been taught about Jesus to a rigorous reexamination and to reflect upon the implications for spiritual integrity in contemporary society.

My personal quest for the authentic Jesus began at the same time that I started to confront the problematic nature of theism and the appeal of alternative forms of Christian spirituality. Eventually, I entered the Roman Catholic community, feeling a deep affinity for the intellectual, contemplative, social, liturgical, and aesthetic dimensions of the international Catholic ethos. Despite my long-standing enchantment with Catholic myth, I have never been convinced that the orthodox synthesis of the Councils of Nicea and Chalcedon adequately does justice to the mystery of God or the person of Jesus. From my perspective, the official two-nature, Trinitarian Christology of creedal Christianity represents only one approach to a set of perennial questions, not a foreclosure on Christological debate. Today, while I cherish my hard-won Catholic identity and my association with the classical heritage of Catholic civilization, my own vision of Christ betrays the influence of a number of different forces—some from the broad range of Christian intellectual life, others from global wisdom traditions outside of Christianity. I continue to consider myself "Catholic" as a way of locating myself on the religious landscape, but I freely modify the proper noun with adjectives such as "agnostic" and "pluralist," always profoundly conscious of both the need for theological humility and the universalist tendencies embedded in the nontribal sense of the term *catholic*.

When it comes strictly to matters of Christology, the term *unitarian* nicely captures the humanist quality of my current approach to Jesus and the unfinished character of my reflections on his ultimate relevance. What started in my adolescent "dark night of the soul" has developed into a lifelong project. Critical readings of the New Testament, the legacy of Protestant liberalism, historical investigations into the first-century milieu, inspiration from Catholic radicalism, and insights from the Asian religious experience have contributed to what is now my working Christology. While rejecting the Nicene-Chalcedonian monopoly on the question of Christ, my Christology-in-progress still retains a bipolar shape, respecting and embracing the finitude of Jesus of Nazareth yet acknowledging his uncanny ability to awaken in others—across a staggering array of centuries and cultures—the transcendent desire for authentic human existence.

When I whispered "Tell me who you are" into the silence of the night nearly three decades ago all of this was in the future. Needless to say, no voice responded to my imperative prayer. But luckily I did have the presence of mind and the common sense to look for answers on my own. Few Southern Baptist youth, or adults for that matter, are prepared to initiate an independent inquiry into the question of Jesus Christ or the literary Christs that confront them in the New Testament texts. The religious literature I knew at the time was largely inspirational or directly tied to pragmatic denominational programs such as missions or church growth. I stumbled across Augustine, Aquinas, Luther, and Wesley and read with great interest portions of the New England Transcendentalist canon in high school. Gradually, it dawned on me that the Christian church had a complex history of development. Family trips to Europe helped to drive home that insight, but I still had no idea that anything such as the historical-critical study of the Bible even existed.

A random examination of commentaries in my church library and on my parents' bookshelves gently introduced me to a level of biblical study beyond sermon preparation and devotional expression. In time I learned what to look for in bookstores—and in which bookstores. My first significant guide to "higher criticism" was the popular Scottish preacher and professor William Barclay, whose Daily Study Bible Series still serves to bridge the gap between academic biblical scholarship and the curious, generally conservative lay reader. From Barclay I learned a number of fundamental points integral to New Testament interpretation lessons that seem so elementary now but until then had completely escaped my notice: the literary/theological character of the Gospel documents themselves (distinguishing them from eyewitness reports); the comprehensive Jewishness of Jesus and his lifestyle and worldview; and the indisputable centrality of the "reign of God" as the conceptual core of Jesus' original message (as opposed to a prototype of what would become Christian doctrine).

Barclay's *The Mind of Jesus* and later his autobiography not only acquainted me with the basics of historical-critical methodology but facilitated my first significant encounter with a respected Christian leader who openly denied the Virgin Birth and confessed an agnostic attitude toward the resurrection. My first real-life meeting with a "unitarian" Christian occurred around the same time. Early in my freshman year of college, I was deeply impressed when my university's chaplain, affiliated with the Disciples of Christ, used that adjective to identify his personal Christological position.

As I moved from Barclay to more serious exemplars of biblical criticism, the hitherto unknown world of liberal Protestant theology opened dramatically before me. Brief forays into Bultmann and the aims of demythologization coincided with my first university-level courses in religious studies. These events naturally led to sporadic but richly rewarding reading in the works of the giants of the twentieth-century liberal establishment: Paul Tillich, Dietrich Bonhoeffer, John A. T. Robinson, John Macquarrie, and Harvey Cox, among others. Bonhoeffer's question of "who Christ really is for us today" struck me forcefully, confirming my original Christological intuition. The Death-of-God theologians from the 1960s, Thomas J. J. Altizer and William Hamilton, also had a tremendous impact. Reading their frank analysis of the eclipse of God in modern experience, I found it remarkable that they continued to see Jesus as the central figure in their theological project. Rereading some of their seminal essays recently, I came across this passage in Hamilton's profile of the modern American theologian called "Thursday's Child," which I first read in the autumn of 1979:

> In Christology, the theologian is sometimes inclined to suspect that Jesus Christ is best understood as neither the object nor the ground of faith . . . but simply as a place to be, a standpoint. That place is, of course, alongside the neighbor, being for him. This may be the meaning of Jesus' true humanity and it may even be the meaning of his divinity, and thus of divinity itself. In any case, now—even when he knows so little about what to believe—he does know where to be.

Today I am amazed at how accurately that passage (despite its sexist language) captured the unusual dynamics of my own spiritual experience at the time—unusual given that I was intensely engaged in church work and determined to enter seminary in a few months. God was undeniably receding in my theological imagination. Jesus, on the other hand, remained a prime concern—a preoccupation and "place to be," if not exactly a model.

All of which is not to say that a definitive portrait of Jesus existed in my mind. My acquaintance with the various quests for the historical Jesus precluded any such Christological confidence. Hugh J. Schonfield's controversial bestseller *The Passover Plot* was my first contact with the scholarly attempt to recover "the man behind the myth." Later I would seek out more rigorous, less speculative ventures in this field, but Schonfield's provocative portrayal of a thoroughly human, visionary Jesus driven by "intense messianic faith," who orchestrated his own crucifixion and (unsuccessful) resurrection, was exactly what I needed to shake me out of my dogmatic slumber. Schonfield was also the first writer to alert me to the anti-Judaic elements in the Gospel narratives. Inspired by his impressive, albeit flawed, achievement, I wrote my first major college paper in religious studies on two problems in the interpretation of Jesus of Nazareth: the question of the reliability of the New Testament texts and the concept of Jesus as the son of God.

Albert Schweitzer demonstrated the brilliance and even nobility of an academically responsible attempt to reconstruct the Jesus of history. His emphasis upon the eschatological thrust of Jesus' mission revolutionized my understanding of the more obscure sayings and actions recorded in the canonical Gospels. His honest description of the historical Jesus as "a stranger and an enigma" to the modern mind only reinforced the countercultural trajectory of my evolving Christology. Over the years, I have returned many times to the famous last paragraph of *The Quest of the Historical Jesus,* in which Schweitzer speaks movingly of the commanding presence and "ineffable mystery" of the Jesus who "comes to us as One unknown."

Since Schweitzer, the enterprise of historical Jesus studies has changed a great deal. Leading figures in the so-called third quest have challenged his exclusive focus on eschatology and expanded the role of archaeology and anthropology in the scholarly project. They have also made enormous use of the Dead Sea Scrolls and the Nag Hammadi Library's Gnostic texts that were not available in Schweitzer's day. What has not been surpassed, in my opinion, is Schweitzer's ability to articulate the enduring relevance of a human Jesus for post-Enlightenment Christians. In another well-known passage, he painted the unforgettable image of "the mangled body of the one immeasurably great Man" tragically crushed by the "wheel of the world" that he helped to set in motion. This is the heroic Jesus whose legacy inspired Schweitzer to renounce a promising career in academics for medical missionary service in French Equatorial Africa and whose "religion of love" laid the groundwork for his philosophy of "reverence for life," which earned him the Nobel Peace Prize. Paradoxically, it is the same sort of Jesus that I would discover in the literature of the Catholic radical tradition. Just about the time that *Superstar* and *Godspell* were revealing unexpected avenues for Christological reflection, I came under the spell of Zeffirelli's *Brother Sun, Sister Moon,* a highly romantic account of the lives of Saint Francis and his female counterpart, Saint Clare. I chanced upon a peaceful sidewalk demonstration outside a London theater where the movie was playing. Long-haired hippies in white robes and bare feet were pacing back and forth in silence, carrying picket signs that read "Live like Saint Francis." A strange juxtaposition of counterculture and the cult of the saints, the sight triggered something in my adolescent imagination. I intuitively knew that this peculiar scene had something to do with my larger search for a meaningful Jesus. From that moment on, a vision of Jesus gradually unfolded in my mind that was dramatically at odds with the culturally domesticated image of Christ accepted by my middle-class American church. This emerging Jesus was very much a contradiction—not only a weird hybrid Jesus (part *Superstar,* part *Passover Plot*) but also an independent and untamed Jesus who told his disciples to transform their lives by leaving their families, selling their possessions, and loving their enemies. Only later would I learn that Francis himself had once been called the *alter Christus,* the other Christ.

What I gained from my acquaintance with the Franciscan tradition was an abiding appreciation for the cardinal place of poverty, homelessness, celibacy, and nonviolence in the mission of Jesus and early Christian discipleship. Everything I read about Francis suggested that he was one of the few people in Christian history who had taken seriously the daunting task of *imitatio Christi.* An unbiased reading of the New Testament gave me all the evidence I needed. Once I began to look for poverty and pacifism in the Gospels, they seemed to appear everywhere. The Sermon on the Mount took on new life and power. What had previously functioned as the repository of devotional platitudes suddenly became the source of a liberating nonconformity that challenged and even subverted the values of mainstream society.

From Francis, I went on to discover the Anabaptists, the Quakers, and a variety of other alternative and "underground" Christianities dedicated to a life of Christ-like simplicity and solidarity. Tolstoy introduced me to a fascinating array of sometimes eccentric intellectuals and activists convinced that the Christ of the Gospels was incompatible with the materialism and violence of conventional culture. Some professed "low" Christologies, while others remained committed to a Christology "from above." Nicea's "high" Christology had become largely discredited for me because of its heavy investment in limited Hellenistic philosophical categories and its political ties to a Constantinian Christendom that subordinated Christ to Caesar.

In college and seminary I was delighted to find representatives of this countercultural impulse in my own tradition. Martin Luther King Jr., Clarence Jordan, Will Campbell, and a handful of others showed me that at least a certain strain in the Baptist heritage had attempted to preserve the disturbing memory of Jesus' anti-imperial critique of wealth and power. Donald Dayton, Ronald Sider, and Jim Wallis directed me to similar currents in the larger evangelical community. Ultimately, I found in the Catholic radical tradition the appealing mix of sacramental spirituality and engaged social consciousness that most effectively nourished my understanding of the potency of Jesus' message.

The movement's emphasis on the preferential option for the poor and a "seamless garment" ethic of life profoundly enlarged the scope of the prophetic Christology taking shape in my imagination. Trappist monk Thomas Merton and the founders of the Catholic Worker movement, Dorothy Day and Peter Maurin, offered inspiring models of what a Franciscan-style awareness of the radicality of Jesus would look like in an age of capitalist consumerism, bourgeois conformism, racial conflict, and superpower competition. I cannot claim to even come close to living up to their standards, but I have returned to their insights many times over the years. Maurin encouraged Christian scholars to "blow the dynamite of the Church." Today I think that means being bold enough and humble enough to recognize the explosive implications of Jesus' message for all facets of life.

A final contributing factor to my ongoing exploration in Christology is a deep immersion in Asian religious thought and practice. Ever since a high school reading of Hermann Hesse's *Siddhartha,* I have been attuned to the beauty, style, and wisdom of classical Asian traditions, especially Hinduism and Buddhism. I was a pluralist and a universalist long before I had the intellectual equipment to define or defend a vision of the transcendent unity of religions. Travel in Asia, training in Zen practice, and professional participation in local and international interfaith dialogue would later confirm these early native intuitions. As Schweitzer once observed, the problem with Christianity is that it "has been so terribly unfaithful to the spirit of Jesus." My experience has taught me that Christians can learn a great deal about the extraordinary spirit of Jesus from sources quite distant from the Christian tradition.

Nothing is particularly new about this idea. Sympathetic Asian readers have always gravitated toward what their Christian counterparts find least attractive in the New Testament: the poverty, celibacy, homelessness, and nonviolence of Jesus. They have also drawn attention to something routinely ignored by pragmatic Westerners: the key place of contemplative silence and solitude in the ministry of Jesus. Long before any Christian theologian commenced the quest for the "unknown Christ of Hinduism," Swami Vivekananda made a forceful case for the unknown Christ of Christianity. Mahatma Gandhi reacquainted many Christians, most notably Martin Luther King Jr., with the forgotten Jesus of the Sermon on the Mount. More recently, the Dalai Lama and Vietnamese exile Thich Nhat Hanh have expressed keen interest in exploring the Buddhist faces of Jesus—especially for the benefit of their spiritually starved Christian admirers.

My own exposure to non-Christian experiments in Christology has dramatically reconfirmed for me the monastic roots of the primitive Jesus movement and the rich interiority of the original Gospel message. Never again will I be able to read the New Testament and disregard the centrality of renunciation, contemplation, nonviolence, and compassion in the way of Jesus. Nor can I imagine seriously entertaining any exercise in Christology that divorces the study of Jesus from issues of personal practice and spiritual experience. Asian reflections on Jesus have also revealed the genuine universality of the Christological enterprise itself. Jesus remains the heart of the Christological project, while Christology shows fewer and fewer indications of being centered exclusively in Christianity. As Jaroslav Pelikan put it in his classic *Jesus Through the Centuries,* "Jesus of Nazareth may have been a provincial, but Jesus Christ is the Man Who Belongs to the World."

The human Jesus of Nazareth continues to arrest my imagination, stimulate my curiosity, and command my respect, even my allegiance—without limiting the horizon of my theological vision. At the same time, the larger, mythic figure of Christ, whose myriad portraits are found in Christianity's own vast internal pluralism and also in countless spiritualities far from the boundaries of Christian tradition, actually expands that horizon and urges me to continue a quest that has now become second nature.

It has been a long time since I implored Jesus to "tell me who you are." My understanding of prayer no longer allows for the issuing of demands or even the posing of questions to invisible supernatural entities. I am glad it once did, though, for it launched one of the greatest adventures of my life. For now, as a self-proclaimed UU Catholic, I stand before the open question of Jesus, marveling as I have many times over the last few decades at Schweitzer's uncanny ability to capture the yearnings of all Christological seekers:

He comes to us as One unknown, without a name,
as of old, by the lakeside, He came to those men who
knew Him not. He speaks to us the same word: "Follow thou me!" and sets us to the tasks which He has
to fulfill for our time. He commands. And to those
who obey Him, whether they be wise or simple,
He will reveal Himself in the toils, the conflicts,
the sufferings which they shall pass through in His
fellowship, and, as an ineffable mystery, they shall
learn in their own experience Who He is.

◄o►

PETER HUFF, *who attends All Souls Unitarian Universalist Church in Shreveport, Louisiana, holds the Thomas Lewis James chair in religious studies at Centenary College. He is author of* Allen Tate and the Catholic Revival *and co-editor of* Knowledge and Belief in America.

Learning to
Love the Questions

CRICKET POTTER

I came to the UU tradition out of a deep anger and hurt over what I experienced in the Presbyterian Church in the late 1980s and early 1990s. I was a divinity student at the time, preparing for ministry in the Presbyterian Church. I thrived on biblical studies, finding a wonderful liberating power in reading the Bible in its original language and studying its stories and lessons within a historical and social context. I delved into social justice issues, feeling compelled by the model and life Jesus offered us and motivated by the readings in our ethics classes. Above all, I learned to love asking the questions I never would have thought to ask from my earlier spoon-fed days of faith and church learning.

Yet once outside the hotbed atmosphere of learning at seminary, I could not ask these same questions within the church setting, or in the larger church body itself. What about social justice and the church's growing stance against gay ordination? What about the violence of the cross and the redemption theology that embraces the cross and the suffering it stands for? Should our communion service really be about Christ's flesh and blood, an understanding that, even as a minister-in-training, I would have been hard-pressed to explain to anyone who asked? Or is it about being in community, breaking bread together, and giving thanks for one another and for the life of Jesus? How can we say in public that we accept the growing religious pluralism of this world and the many paths up the mountain while in church we hold tight to the belief that we, as Christians, are the only true body of Christ, the only ones who know the right path up the mountain?

So I left the Presbyterian Church, unsure of whether I could call myself a Christian anymore and doubtful that I could ever find a church home that would feel comfortable and welcoming, given my proclivity for questions.

It was springtime in New England when I first walked into what would soon become my new church home. The sanctuary was awash with the morning light, large sprigs of cherry blossoms and pussy willows adorned the pulpit area, where the only religious symbols were a simple chalice and a brightly adorned quilt hanging displaying the many symbols of the world's religions on the wall behind the pulpit. From the call to worship and the chalice lighting to the pastoral prayer and the sermon, I heard God spoken of in a wonderfully inclusive and freeing way: spirit of life, source of our being, breath of our breaths, hope of hopes, and the power of creation that moves in, among, and through all of creation. Something deep within me that had been pushed shut was suddenly flung open as I was allowed, encouraged even, to imagine the divine in new and creative ways.

In the weeks that followed, I came to anticipate each Sunday at this UU church with great joy, looking forward to new ways of learning about and experiencing the sacred. I was like a moth drawn to a flame as I came to appreciate the place reason and experience held in the UU tradition. My questions and personal interpretation were supported and often echoed by others. I was, in the words of the poet Rilke, thriving in living the questions.

After eleven years, I have developed a deep love and respect for this tradition that I have claimed as my own, even as I see and understand more and more clearly its weaknesses and shortcomings. No UU church can explicitly meet all my spiritual needs, Christian or otherwise. Nor do I expect it to, just as I wouldn't expect my life partner to meet all my personal needs. What I do experience, however, is a creating, sustaining, and challenging faith that, in Rev. Rosemary Bray McNatt's words, "gives me faith in life and courage for life."

As a Christian UU, I may be a small fish in a big pond. But we UUs all share the values upheld in our Principles and Purposes, and they are the bedrock of my Christian faith and life today. Certainly, I would like to lift up our Judeo-Christian roots more, and I would like the Bible and Jesus to be less troublesome concepts within our congregations and more a source of inspiration and guidance. I can live with that, though. What gives me hope and adds depth to my personal faith, as well as my faith in our tradition, is how we live out what Jesus modeled for us and what the Bible calls us to do, even if we don't frame it that way. I am so proud of the stand our tradition has taken over the years on issues of justice. As a resident of Massachusetts, I loved witnessing firsthand the vocal and strong stand our churches and the Unitarian Universalist Association of Congregations took on the issue of same-sex marriage. Weeks after the momentous court decision supporting same-sex marriage, I wept when I received a wedding invitation that pictured a towel rack with two towels on it, both monogrammed with the word *hers*.

My hope is that we always strive to see past the labels we tend to put on one another, that we avoid the "othering" we can easily slip into when we don't see eye-to-eye theologically, and that we celebrate the essence of what we share in a tradition rich with dialogue and diversity steeped in an unshakable understanding of the inherent worth and dignity of all human beings, whatever their beliefs.

―◦―

CRICKET POTTER *received a master of divinity degree from San Francisco Theological Seminary in 1992 as a Presbyterian. She is currently serving as a ministerial intern at the First Parish in Lincoln, Massachusetts.*

Pain, Psalm, Prayer
and a Promise

RON ROBINSON

As I was growing up, Jesus was a constant figure in my life, but he seemed out of reach. He was divine, someone to try to measure up to, but to whom of course I could never measure up. Jesus was submerged within the more intimate reality of "the church," which was not the Church Universal but my local Methodist church, full of family, neighbors, and teachers. Back then I didn't understand that the church embodied, however imperfectly, Jesus in the world and in my life. I only knew that there was a disconnect between the church that nurtured me and the "God and His Son" it asked me to believe in.

Still, I was a youth leader. I organized Jesus marches, wrote a church newsletter column, and helped found a youth choir. One Sunday evening I even led a service and preached. Looking back, I should have known a departure was coming when I based my text for that Sunday evening sermon in Turley, Oklahoma, in the early 1970s on Abbie Hoffman's book *Revolution for the Hell of It*. I know now that my intent was to hold up the revolutionary spirit of Jesus. But at the time I thought it was an attempt to speak to the countercultural movement (not that there was much of it present in Turkey) and to say, "Jesus did this too, so pay attention to others who are doing it today." Today my mission is to lift up Jesus' liberation story as countercultural and revolutionary for both those who want nothing to do with him and for those who have tried to control him for their own political, institutional, or dogmatic purposes.

When I was seventeen, a good friend was killed in a car collision right before Christmas. For the first time I began to seriously ponder the Big Questions of heaven and hell and immortality. I questioned whether Jesus is the only way to salvation, which led me to question what Christianity, as a Jesus religion, was all about. I left my church and family to go to college, further alienating myself from the religion of my childhood. At college, I experimented with new ideas, making my way among Mormons for a while, and then Bahais. I immersed myself in Eastern philosophy and then turned my focus to politics. But I couldn't leave Jesus completely behind.

When I first encountered Unitarianism through my studies of nineteenth-century American literature, I felt a new doorway open up. Emerson, Channing, and Parker were right in synch with where I was at the time. They couldn't leave Jesus behind either, but they seemed to me, in those first encounters with their work anyway, to be keeping Jesus safely away from where the real action, real religion, was taking place. This was just right for me.

Soon after college, I began my life within the Unitarian church. Jesus receded even further into my spiritual closet. As a UU I could experience the community intimacy of my childhood church without any theological crises. Every once in a while I'd let Jesus out of the closet briefly, but only as a kind of reminder of why I'd stowed him away in the first place. (See, Jesus, what others are saying in your name? This is why you go back on the top shelf).

I became a Unitarian because the Jesus of my childhood had been a distant object of my early religious focus. The church's creed about him seemed intent on restricting my soul's liberty. But even though I was embracing the freedom of Unitarianism now, Jesus remained distant. In Jewish theologian Martin Buber's words, my religion was all I-it instead of I-Thou, in both my childhood and early UU experience as an adult. When I was younger the spiritual focus was on Jesus as an "it," an object of worship. As a UU, I was wrapped up in myself. But the self, the "I," quickly becomes an object itself without authentic interaction.

In ways I wouldn't see until later, paths were opening up for me in my early UU years that would allow Jesus and me to walk together—for the first time. One of these was the power of story. As a writer, editor, reporter, reader, and film freak, I was immersed in narratives of meaning.

I came to realize that stories and symbols shape lives, and the stories I encountered anew in the Bible began to shape me like no others. Now I see the Bible stories as full of lives struggling with God and the world's powers and with each other and their own conflicted selves. Hearing UU process theologian Charles Hartshorne speak at my church on "Taking Freedom Seriously" opened up another path and a new understanding of God. His talk captivated my imagination and led me to much deeper theological reflection on how God could be seen as active in the world. Jesus wasn't yet visible on either of these paths, but when you walk the paths called Story and God, you often meet Jesus at the intersection.

Here came Jesus, in pain and in psalms.

I started a UU church in the small Oklahoma town of Tahlequah in 1991. In order to answer more fully the questions of others about our faith and its tradition, I began reading more deeply in our Unitarian and Universalist histories about the men and women who bravely stood for a different way of being Christian than the prevailing ways of their times. Their lives and words and churches provided roots, and I began to see the presence and vision of a Jesus who offered a window to God through his own life, words, and ministry, and his radical sense of community. About this time I joined the UU Christian Fellowship to begin learning more, even though I didn't yet think of calling myself a Christian. At this time my relationship with Jesus was entirely of the mind, as it had been when I was young.

I had also started a family. During this time one of my children had to be in the hospital often. I remember taking a break from the neonatal ICU room where we'd been for several days and just sitting in the car in the parking garage. I wasn't praying. But I put in a tape from Sweet Honey in the Rock; it was as if I were letting someone else pray for me. A gospel music of hope lifted me up and sent me back inside. At another hospital, after another surgery and a particularly bad post-surgery period, I found myself repeating from memory the children's story *Goodnight Moon* over and over again. It became the prayer I said to bring peace and comfort and sleep to my child. Seated on a hard hospital-room chair I felt the need to escape into some other kind of reading. There in the drawer was the Bible. I stopped flipping pages when I reached the Psalms and began to listen as I read, feeling more deeply than ever before the old story of suffering and exile and thanksgiving and renewal and feeling a part of a continuous community of souls. I'd found my story. Not my answers, but my story. I was meeting Jesus' God through the body, exhausted, and through the Spirit, fearful.

Here came Jesus, in prayer.

Soon after, in my work as a campus ministry coordinator, I heard a talk on daily meditation based on the Lord's Prayer by a Catholic faculty member. I tried it myself and have maintained it ever since. Even though the prayer is addressed to God (or Abba, Father-Mother, or Creative Parent), the daily repetition of some of the oldest words ascribed to Jesus and found meaningful by his followers brought me closer to him. At first I focused so much of my meditation on the meaning of the words, wrestling with them, not believing them, but repeating them nonetheless over and over, eventually letting them simply enter my being. As the days, weeks, months, and now years have gone by, the words have become as much a part of me as breathing. They are my wellspring in moments of anxiety or pain. When I started this prayer, I was still uneasy thinking of myself as a Christian, but I'd found my prayer and a sustaining spiritual practice.

Jesus, in parable and in purpose.

After I began my spiritual practice with the Lord's Prayer, I attended a weekend retreat seminar, hosted by Hope Unitarian Church in Tulsa, that focused on the parables of Jesus and was led by seminary professor Brandon Scott, a member of the Jesus Seminar. The radical power of those subversive parable gems called me, as they had to Jesus, to reimagine and reorient my life toward the "kingdom or kin-dom of God or G-d," and to discover deeper purpose, to go where God, not the world, was leading me. This process helped lead me into seminary and a commitment to a life of service, striving to imitate and initiate such a "kindom." For the first time I began describing myself as a

Christian, regardless of how other UUs or more orthodox Christians might respond. I'm still not fully comfortable doing so and may never be, but I seek to grow more into an understanding of what that might mean.

Jesus, in a people.

In seminary, I fell in love with the newly emerging perspectives on Paul, our earliest known witness of Jesus' life. I felt a deep affinity for this soul who'd had his own complicated relationship with Jesus in his sometimes conflicting faith communities. Paul and many of the other early followers of Jesus were Jews who hadn't left the Torah behind, though they found fulfillment anew in how the God of Israel had acted through Jesus to usher in a new way of relating to him. In following Jesus' faithfulness, Paul and others found themselves on, in, and between the margins as Jews, Jesus-followers, and people steeped in Roman-Greco culture.

So too I found myself still deeply connected to Unitarian Universalism, which had broadened beyond the Christianity of its birth. In some ways my ties to Unitarian Universalism were even stronger than my ties to mainstream Christianity because I had discovered my truer, deeper relationship with Jesus as a UU. I hadn't left freedom, non-creedalism, and a love for diversity behind when I became a new kind of Christian, as had Paul, who became a new kind of Jew; indeed, I felt myself more deeply attached to them than ever before. My theological touchstones were threefold.

The first was that God works in freedom, and to know or experience what I call God requires the freedom to think, choose, doubt, and change. The growth of the soul is only possible in the soil of liberty (or as Paul says in 2 Corinthians 3:17, "Where the Spirit of the Lord is, there is liberty"). I haven't found a better place to live in the story of freedom than Unitarian Universalism.

My central story of freedom is the liberating biblical story of Jesus, another touchstone for me. God is present there, but he is also present in other great stories of freedom found in science, philosophy, art, and humanities; in other religions; and in people's contemporary lives. Unitarian Universalism brings me into contact with all of the myriad ways God speaks to us today.

Finally, to really follow in the spirit of Jesus means to be in right relationship with those who are different from me, to find mutual healing and transformation in such relationships. In Unitarian Universalism I have many rich opportunities for such encounters.

Despite my growing devotion to Unitarian Universalism, I was now in a theological minority because I was also growing more deeply connected to the worldwide faith community of Christianity, even with the creedal Christianity that had rejected Unitarians and Universalists before we rejected it. My theological touchstones are often tested by UUs and Christians who do not share them, who do not see and feel a great abundance in them but instead react from what strikes me as a sense of scarcity and a fear of real difference, of conflict. At the deepest level, I sense a fear of particularity. The more at home I felt with Jesus within the UU Church and vice versa, and the more I expressed it, the more my conversations with others developed an edge. I would say that my faith was one of being "particular, but not exclusive," but people seemed to hear exclusion in my words. With other UUs, it was as if we had traded the freedom and responsibility of the spiritual search, our hallmark, for the desire not to be settled. With other Christians, it was as if Jesus didn't mean what he said about the Great Commandment and true neighbors (Luke 10:25-37), as if Christianity began with Augustine, was refined by Aquinas, and found its fulfillment in Calvin.

Just as I had been changing spiritually and theologically over the years, so too had Unitarian Universalism, Christianity. Neither was UU Christianity the same as it had been in the times of Ballou, Channing, Emerson, Parker, Gannett, Bellows, or Eliot. It had even changed significantly from what it was in 1945, when the Unitarian Universalist Christian Fellowship was founded.

The more I learn of the diverse and rapidly changing first century in Palestine and other areas of the Roman Empire, where Paul journeyed and preached about his unitarian and universalist experience of Jesus, the more it seems like the early twenty-first century. In many ways Jesus was experienced then, as now, as the Christ. For Paul Christ began as a personal experience (the apocryphal "road to Damascus" vision), but Christ developed into a communal experience—the spread of the house church, the letters about how to live as Christ inclusively in community, the hope that soon the world would be transformed. Jesus was present in all of that. What had begun as a personal experience of forming a relationship with Jesus as a kind of mental and emotional lens to God has deepened as I experience the spirit of Jesus in community. I witness the birth of new churches, new small groups of Jesus—followers, new events like the annual UUCF Revival, new online communities, and new relationships. Jesus said, "Wherever two or more are gathered in my name, there I am."

At age fifty it seems I have come full circle—finding Jesus in community and in the church whose mission is to be the church outside itself, and in its practices and people, incomplete and broken. When I was young I heard the name Jesus everywhere but could experience him nowhere. Now I experience Jesus virtually everywhere, all the time, in the least of moments as well as the encounters with the "least of these" (Matthew 25). Even when the least of these is myself. My relationship with Jesus has been strengthened not so much by all these years and experiences of evolving understandings and new insights, as important as they have been, as much as through my missteps, my broken relationships and covenants, my failures to live up to my potential and my responsibilities as a father, husband, citizen, minister, and child of God. The dominant powers of my time and place have sought, and sometimes found success, in making an "object" of me on the varied crosses of life. When I have not taken my freedom and the covenants upon which freedom is founded and forged seriously enough, I still find Jesus, the resurrected one, the one who is free of the cross, whose spirit lived beyond the cross and became deeper within others, calling to me again, to join him and others again, to follow after him among others again. He continues going ahead of us on the road to Emmaus (Luke 24:13-35), the road to Galilee (Mark 16:1-8), and the road of my life, re-covenanting with me in the possibilities of amazing and everlasting grace.

Jesus, in pain and psalm and prayer and parable and purpose and a people and always in a promise.

―o―

RON ROBINSON *is the executive director of the Unitarian Universalist Christian Fellowship and works at Epiphany Church just outside Tulsa, Oklahoma, helping to start new churches.*

3-D Jesus

KATHLEEN ROLENZ

All theology is autobiography. In a way, my story about how I "came to Jesus" is unique and entirely my own; in another way, it's a story I've heard told many times. The details may be different, but the results are the same. But first, a bit of background.

I grew up attending a Missouri Synod Lutheran Church for the first thirteen years of my life. It's not because my family were devout Lutherans, quite the contrary. Years later I was told that my parents dropped us off at Sunday School so that they could have some "alone" time on Sunday morning. I liked the Lutheran Church school, with its felt-board cutouts of a white Jesus holding little lambs, but never thought much about Jesus or church or God when I wasn't there. When I was thirteen I had what you could call my first "crisis of faith." I was attending confirmation class at the Lutheran Church with Pastor Beale. That particular Wednesday night, he was stressing the importance of baptism. He told us about a mother whose baby had recently died. He told that mother that her baby was not going to heaven because she had neglected to have him baptized before he died. I remember blurting out to Pastor Beale, "That's wrong! What a terrible thing to say to somebody about their baby!" Pastor Beale was furious and forbade me to come back to confirmation class until he had spoken with my mother. But when he called and explained what had happened, my mother said the same thing I did and made him so mad that he hung up on her! After that, I didn't go back to church. I began my long journey toward atheism, nihilism, and agnosticism, until I found a UU church in college.

In 1983 I was very much an existentialist agnostic. It was a good fit. I didn't have to deal with God or Jesus or the Bible in my little UU church because the topic never came up. When I felt a call to the ministry, it wasn't because I felt much of a kinship with God or Christianity. I could happily escape the trappings of the Christian church and focus on a more philosophical or existential approach to religion. God, however, seemed to have other plans.

While serving my first church in Knoxville, Tennessee, I was invited to participate in an ecumenical lectionary study group. They met as a group of clergy colleagues every week to study passages of the Bible with silence, reflection, more silence, and personal experience as it related to the scripture passage. I accepted this invitation not because I was all that interested in the Bible but because I was lonely and desperately needed friends and colleagues with whom

I could just "be." One morning I read a passage from the New Testament with the group, and something happened. Jesus seemed to step out of the page and come alive. Like a three dimensional hologram, I saw that he wasn't a feltboard cutout; nor was he a simple amalgamation of stories and rumors. In that instant, he became flesh and blood to me. Somehow, I *got it—I* got what Jesus was trying to tell us. Then, just as abruptly as I had found him, I lost that initial moment of enlightenment. I have spent the rest of my life looking for that 3-D Jesus.

So who is Jesus to me? As Unitarian Universalists we like to say that Jesus is no greater than all the other prophets or teachers. We liken him to a guru, as in the Buddhist tradition—a wise teacher who is the embodiment of the Bodhisattva or Christ-consciousness. Most UUs would hesitate to call Jesus their "Lord and Savior." Frankly, it's taken me years to feel comfortable with that language, yet oddly enough I now choose to call Jesus my Lord and Savior without hesitation. Why?

First of all, to say that Jesus is "Lord" doesn't mean that I bow down to him as a worthless speck of dust. It means that I acknowledge Jesus as *my* teacher, *my* guru, one who has more knowledge than I. I affirm that there is a greater truth than I can imagine and that Jesus had some insight into that truth. Jesus then becomes more than a teacher to me; he becomes the Christ.

I also used to feel uncomfortable with the word *Christ.* In one sermon I joked that "Christ" was *not* Jesus' last name!

However, now I believe that the word *Christ* defines a term of respect—not unlike the titles we give professors, doctors, or ministers. If Jesus, then, is "the Christ," what does that mean? Along with that, what does Jesus Christ as "Savior" mean to me? Does it mean he "died for my sins," as the term is so commonly understood? My answer to that is "yes, and no." I don't believe that Jesus gave his life to eradicate my original sin. That's a theology I just cannot buy. However, what inspires me about Jesus—what enables me to say both yes *and* no—is that Jesus died because people were not able to bear their own self-hatred. Jesus was a mirror to people. They saw in him who they truly are. Jesus had this uncanny ability to see people for who they are and to love them anyway. I believe that it was the ugliness that people saw in themselves—the hatred, bigotry, prejudice, and fears—that ultimately killed Jesus. Jesus has been my "savior" by serving as a role model of how I want to behave. Jesus saves me when I refuse to assign evil motives to others and believe in their essential goodness instead. Jesus saves me when I am able to put my own ego out of the way and simply be present to another human being. Jesus saves me from sin—not because he died for me, but because he lived in the light of love for others.

So, who needs Jesus? I believe the secular world needs Jesus. I speak with many newcomers to West Shore Unitarian Universalist Church in Cleveland who are hoping to participate in a larger story. Many come from a Christian background but they are not necessarily rejecting Christianity or their upbringing. Many newcomers have had little or no church background. They have seen the values of the secular world and *they want something more.* At the same time, they don't have issues with Christianity. They simply want to find a church that will allow them to explore this larger story regardless of where it takes them.

Unitarian Universalists need Jesus, too. First of all, we need to connect with our own history. We wouldn't be here if it weren't for Jesus. We neglect our own history at our peril. We also must become more comfortable with traditional religious language. We must be able to speak the language of another's religious tradition without hesitation or fear. We don't want to be a marginalized faith on the world's stage. And finally, I believe we must genuinely embrace the religious diversity of our own church members—including the Christians among us.

My congregation has historically leaned toward humanist beliefs and practices. Initially, members were reluctant to call a self-identified, out-of-the-closet Christian Unitarian Universalist to serve them. Since they did, the congregation has been asking questions about my faith and wants to engage in further conversation about what Christianity means to me, who or what God is for me, and who or what Jesus is for me. I applaud their courage. They have discovered that their Christian UU minister has not suddenly turned fundamentalist on them. Instead, they realize the truth of our forebear Francis David's words when he wrote, "We need not think alike, to love alike." To my surprise and delight, we've discovered common ground based on the very principles of nonjudgmentalism, truth-telling, and love exhibited by my teacher, Jesus.

―◦―

KATHLEEN ROLENZ *is on the Board of Trustees of the Unitarian Universalist Christian Fellowhip and she serves as editor of* Good News, *the quarterly publication of the Fellowship. With her husband, Wayne Arnason, she is parish co-minister at the West Shore Unitarian Universalist Church in Cleveland, Ohio.*

A Mad Mix of
Dedicated People

JOHN SIMCOX

I first visited a Unitarian church as a college student in Minneapolis in 1956. In the early sixties, I found a home in the humanist congregation of the First Unitarian Society in Minneapolis. I wanted to be as far removed from my ancestral Lutheranism as possible.

In 1970, living in New York City, I found myself increasingly drawn to spiritual exploration. After a period of church hopping, I settled into the Unitarian Church of All Souls. I savored classes in the historical Jesus, Unitarian history, and world religions taught by its minister, Walter Donald Kring. The version of the Bond of Union that was used in those days seemed especially meaningful to me: In the freedom of the truth and in the spirit of Jesus we unite for the worship of God and the service of man.

I returned to Minnesota in 1978 after fourteen years in New York. I'd become fond of Unitarianism and Universalism at All Souls, but the UU churches I visited in the Twin Cities encompassed neither. As I'd been a student of New Thought literature during my New York years, I became affiliated with a local New Thought church for more than twenty years. I found both Unitarianism (understood as oneness of God) and Universalism (as in universal salvation) in many New Thought writings, and the Jesus that appeared in some of these writings seemed to be a sympathetic (if possibly not historic) figure.

So, why did my enthusiasm for New Thought eventually wane? I have often felt that the movement was becoming a prosperity cult. (Henry Wood, a New Thought author in Boston, had been apprehensive about that prospect one hundred years earlier.) Many of my New Thought friends embraced popular culture in ways that I never have. In addition, I became uncomfortable with the radically individualistic sense of identity common among New Thoughters. An impersonal, automatically responsive side of God called "Law" (in addition to the side called "Love") was advanced by New Thought teachers. I wondered about the ways in which Jesus was understood, especially among those who considered him a prosperity teacher.

Increasingly attracted to liberal Protestantism, I looked at the Unitarian Universalist Christian Fellowship website late in 2001, became a member, and now attend the annual revival. My present churchgoing includes both a UU church and a United Church of Christ congregation. I'm among those who would like to see both more Unitarianism and more Universalism in a denomination called Unitarian Universalism.

Some friends have suggested that I am a low-Christology Christian. Although I wouldn't quite call myself a "follower" of Jesus, I wish to live in the spirit of the historical Jesus and also the Jesus I believe lives today, in the way that we all live after our bodily demise. In one way or another, virtually all UU Christians have experienced the spirit of Jesus drawing them to God. Although I do not always know how to apply general principles to particular situations, my ideal is pacifism, and I wish to extend that principle to our relations with nonhuman animals that share the life of the world with us. I believe that the birds, beasts, fishes, and quite possibly other life forms will be included in the final harmony of all souls with God.

There are some problems associated with being a Christian in today's Unitarian Universalism, especially if you reside in a place where UU Christians are virtually nonexistent. But because I cherish the traditions of Unitarianism and Universalism, I am not tempted to leave the denomination. UU Christianity is a movement made up of a mad mix of dedicated people, a fellowship that weaves, flows, and finds its way in spite of indifference, failure, and setback.

Although I am aware of other religious movements that impart unitarian and universalist ideas to a greater extent than our denomination does, I feel that Unitarian Universalism, at least in some respects, provides the most congenial environment and the broadest growth opportunity for Christians like me.

―◦―

JOHN SIMCOX *attends both Unity Church Unitarian in St. Paul, Minnesota, and Lyndale United Church of Christ in Minneapolis. He is also active in the Network of Spiritual Progressives, an interfaith project of the Tikkun Community.*

The Advocate

CAROL STAMATAKIS

I have always felt closest to God and most inspired by Jesus' example when working in the pursuit of justice. In protecting and promoting the civil and human rights of vulnerable people, those who have been historically marginalized in our society, I have most strongly felt the power of God. My longing for a more just world has a source deeper than my Christian upbringing, but Christian teachings helped me to develop that longing and give it voice, shape, and meaning.

The Greek Orthodox Church in which I was raised helped cultivate my spiritual sensitivity. The chanting of the cantor, the ancient Greek language of the liturgy, candles, and incense created a sacred space, set apart from the outside world, that spoke to the mystery of God. But as I approached adolescence, I became deeply troubled over the patriarchal structure of the Church and its emphasis on doctrine. I remember arguing with my Sunday School teacher in the seventh grade. I could not understand how somebody born in a non-Christian country could fairly be expected to adopt Christianity, or why their good deeds did not matter if they were not Christian. Her explanation was that because of all the missionaries in the world, everybody had an opportunity to come to know Christ, and if they did not convert they had only themselves to blame. I recognized this for the absurdity that it was.

I studied sociology in college and became interested in the socioeconomic structure of our society. A class called "Civil Liberties and the Courts" deeply inspired me, and I came to see law as an avenue for societal change. We read and studied U.S. Supreme Court cases, mostly from the Warren era, involving civil liberties and constitutional rights and meant to move our society in the direction of greater justice and compassion. I came to appreciate the interrelationship between social and legal change. But I was more excited by the law's potential to move society toward progress in areas of social and economic justice. So I became a lawyer. I married a fellow law student who shared my political beliefs and personal values, and we moved to rural New Hampshire to live close to nature in an unpretentious small town.

I explored different churches in an effort to find a supportive spiritual community. My first experience with a Unitarian Universalist Church was in 1987, when the women's spirituality curriculum "Cakes for the Queen of Heaven" was offered at the Unitarian Universalist Meeting-house in Ascutney, Vermont. This class was an extremely powerful and affirming experience that brought together my spiritual and political selves. We studied ancient cultures that worshiped female deities and explored the treatment of women in different religious traditions. The class was also experiential in nature, involving the creation of rituals to honor the feminine. Unfortunately, the church closed shortly after the class ended, but I was so inspired by my experience there that I began a deliberate search for another UU church.

I eventually joined the Keene Unitarian Universalist Church. The church members were gentle and kind and seemed to share my values. I created and led a workshop on legal issues affecting gays and lesbians for a regional conference called "Affirming Every Person." The workshop dealt with a historical perspective as well as a discussion of the current state of the law in areas such as housing and employment discrimination. My goal was to show that progress was being made despite setbacks and to inspire participants to keep up the fight and avoid falling into despair. I was extremely gratified to be in a position to use my legal background to provide the participants with encouragement and support.

Spending time with others who shared my political beliefs and values was rewarding, but not enough to sustain me spiritually. The Keene church was humanistic, and I felt frustrated over the careful avoidance of the word *God* during worship and conversation. Church members used the word *Christian* carelessly, usually in a derogatory way, to describe fundamentalists. There seemed to be an understanding that Unitarian Universalists could not be Christian. This was hard for me since it was my search for God that had led me to Unitarian Universalism, and my understanding of God had been significantly informed by the teachings of Jesus, though I studied and drew inspiration from other traditions as well.

Fortunately, I discovered the Unitarian Universalist Christian Fellowship. A poster advertising a UUCF event caught my attention. It depicted many paths up a mountain, symbolizing the Christian path as one of many paths to the divine. This was how I saw my spiritual quest. I respected the other paths, but I was most likely to achieve spiritual growth by choosing and following one path with diligence and an open heart and mind. I attended a UUCF retreat, where there were small group discussions and sessions on prayer practices and spiritual disciplines. The other members were kindred spirits who found inspiration in Christianity, yet they were a diverse group of independent thinkers.

I made efforts to supplement my UU church activities with occasional Christian worship services or Bible studies at other churches. At times I would experience disagreeable dogma, or be unable to express myself openly because I held views that others were likely to see as heretical. I felt as if I were living a double life and not being true to myself in either setting. One Sunday a member of the Keene church apologized to the congregation because the choir sang a song with the word *Lord* in it. I experienced this as a personal rejection, though I did not express this to anyone. I quietly left the church and briefly attended another UU church that was more inclusive theologically. However, it was far from my home and the distance was an issue.

I gave up on the idea that I would find a church that could really meet my needs as both a UU and a Christian and decided to concentrate on pursuing the Christian path. I began attending a Christian church in another denomination that seemed tolerant and friendly. I studied the Bible and attended Bible study classes. I read books on how to apply Christian principles to everyday life and sought to do so in every area of my life. I prayed regularly and found encouragement in biblical passages such as "I can do all things through Christ who strengthens me." I made copies of the Bible passages that inspired me the most, kept them with me, and read them often, along with prayers I'd collected. Some of my favorite passages were those that spoke to social responsibility, such as James 1:27: "Religion that is pure and undefiled before God, the Father, is this: to care for orphans and widows in their distress, and to keep one's self unstained by the world." When faced with challenges, I was able to move forward without fear and with incredible determination. I had struggled with work-related stress for many years and was finally able to overcome it as a result of these spiritual practices.

I read books on the historical Jesus and educated myself about the origins of church-created doctrines that I had experienced as a barrier to spiritual understanding. I was able to abandon them or at least ease the fear and confusion they generated. I sometimes used resources written by conservative Christians who expressed views that I disagreed with. I was able to recognize the intrinsic wisdom of their ideas and apply them despite our theological differences. I noticed that many "Christian" principles were the same as those found in Buddhism and other traditions, but within the context of Jesus' teachings and my growing understanding of God's power and love, as informed by the Jewish and Christian traditions, they made a far greater impression on me than they would have if I had randomly dabbled in different religions without the depth of understanding my narrower focus allowed.

I worked in a private law practice and served on various boards in my spare time in an effort to support causes I cared about. I wanted to affect public policy more directly, so I ran for the state legislature and served three terms. My years in the legislature were educational, though my efforts met with only modest success, mostly in the area of environmental protection. I was more successful in preventing destructive laws from passing than in getting beneficial legislation through. The competing demands of parenthood and my law practice eventually forced me to give up serving in the legislature. Years later, I was fortunate to find the opportunity to use my legislative experience in advocacy work for elders and people with disabilities. In this capacity I was far more successful than I had ever been as a legislator.

I left private law practice to prosecute child abuse and neglect cases. The work was difficult and fraught with moral ambiguities. I frequently prayed about my cases, asking God to give the judge wisdom or help him or her see the truth rather than for a particular outcome. In order to help me maintain a sense of divine presence, I would often visualize Jesus accompanying me over the course of a day, sitting in courtrooms and watching over children and parents, many of whom had themselves been victims of abuse. Cases were often complicated by poverty, mental illness, intellectual disability, addiction, or domestic violence. Children were sometimes so badly damaged that they did not respond to therapy; they bounced from one foster home to another or grew up in group homes. Saddest of all were the failed adoptions. I frequently turned to the serenity prayer quoted by Reinhold Niebuhr: "God grant me the serenity to accept the things I cannot change; courage to change the things I can; and the wisdom to know the difference. . . . Taking, as He did, this sinful world as it is, not as I would have it."

One time I was involved in the deposition of a woman who had reported her son for child abuse in order to protect her grandchild. I was worried about how she would withstand the legal process, having seen people in similar circumstances collapse under the pressure. I was also concerned about the attorney for the parents, who was known to be aggressive and disrespectful toward opposing parties. During the deposition I visualized Jesus sitting in an empty chair between the woman and myself, and I focused on the comfort and support that this image provided. To my surprise, the woman testified calmly, truthfully, and powerfully. The other attorney was uncharacteristically quiet and respectful. Following the deposition I told the woman that I knew what she had done was very hard, and that I was surprised she had held up as well as she did. She smiled and said that it was easy because Jesus was beside her the whole time.

I later took a position that involved working with the legislature on issues affecting older people and people with disabilities. I helped educate the public about pending legislation and how they could influence the legislative process. My work focused on efforts to strengthen the laws governing elder abuse, financial exploitation, and other mistreatment of vulnerable adults. I applied the knowledge I had gained in previous endeavors, including my years as a legislator. During this time, my spiritual life and legal career were aligned in a way that was more powerful and dynamic than anything I had ever experienced before. I was successful in building coalitions and helping to pass many pieces of legislation.

I have found tremendous meaning and inspiration in the stories of Jesus' miraculous healing of people who probably had mental illnesses or physical disabilities and were regarded as unclean, outcasts in the world they inhabited. I believe Jesus possessed an astounding ability to look past the societal stereotypes, ignorance, and superstition of the time he lived to see all people as they truly were, as whole and complete human beings. Those he touched were able to see themselves through his eyes and were healed.

Jesus' ability to love and accept those who were rejected by his society is staggering in its significance, far more than any supernatural intervention could be. If today we can see these marginalized people as we see ourselves, and treat them as we would treat ourselves, we will inevitably create services and supports to diminish the impact of their disabilities and enable them to live full lives. We can all be healed. I have come to believe, as a result of my work in the areas of child and domestic abuse, that the effects of abuse are often spiritual in nature and can best be addressed if the victims can come to see themselves through God's eyes rather than through the eyes of the perpetrator or their own shame.

Recently, my work has focused on supporting people with disabilities. At a meeting, a woman with a developmental disability told me that she disliked the term "inclusion." Her statement surprised me. She explained that she did not want *inclusion,* she wanted to *belong.* In her experience, the well-intentioned special education programs of her schooling forced others to "include" her in various activities, but she did not really belong. She explained that the only place she has ever experienced true belonging is in her church, where people do not see her disability. Her comments helped me to strive for the more elusive ideal of belonging.

True acceptance of others requires a change of heart. Jesus emphasized what is in one's heart over the complicated religious laws of his day. Evil as well as good begins in the heart. In Matthew 5:27-28 Jesus says, "You have heard it said, 'You shall not commit adultery.' But I say to you that everyone who looks at a woman with lust has already committed adultery with her in his heart." Jesus' Great Commandment (Matthew 22:37-40) states, "You shall love the Lord your God with all of your heart, and with all your soul, and with all your mind. This is the greatest and first commandment. And a second is like it: 'You shall love your neighbor as your self.' On these two commandments hang all the law and the prophets."

Even after I stopped attending a UU church, I continued to see myself as a Unitarian Universalist. On occasion I was confronted with doctrines of the church that I could not accept or that made no sense to me, but I tried not to focus on them. As my children grew older, I wanted them to encounter a broader vision of spirituality and greater diversity. When extreme discord developed over internal matters in my church I was forced to reevaluate my involvement. I discovered that the church was governed by a hierarchy with conflicted interests that was unable to respond to the needs of the local church. I also learned, around the same time, that the United Methodist Church, which had struggled over gay rights for years, had taken a position nationally that was contrary to my own beliefs and values. While I loved the members of the local church, I could not ignore the moral issues inherent in what my financial contributions were supporting. I had been on a long vacation, but it was time to go home.

Ten years had passed since I had been in the Keene Unitarian Universalist Church. Yet I returned, almost instinctively, one Sunday. At that moment, I needed more than anything to be in a spiritually safe place, and I knew the Keene church was that place. I did not know what to expect when I quietly slipped in for worship. I contemplated the stained-glass window, which depicts a person of indeterminate gender in a robe, carrying a lamp to symbolize Truth. I made a commitment at that moment to be honest with myself and with others, and take responsibility for times in the past when I had not done so. I knew that I was where I should be at that moment. I also knew that it was my responsibility to help make a place for myself and other UU Christians. I quickly learned that the church had changed in my absence and now seemed much more inclusive theologically. Or maybe I had changed. I could not be sure.

In the Gospel of John (14:15-17), Jesus tells his disciples that the time is drawing near when he will no longer be with them, but reassures them that they will not be alone. "And I will ask the Father, and he will give you another Advocate, to be with you forever. This is the Spirit of truth, whom the world cannot receive, because it neither sees him nor knows him. You know him, because he abides with you, and he will be among you." He gives them his peace and tells them not to let their hearts be troubled or be afraid.

One of the many words used to describe the Holy Spirit is *advocate*. As a lawyer I am of course an advocate. In this sense the Holy Spirit is like having a really good lawyer around! My work has been the most inspired and godly when I am functioning as an advocate for the interests of elders and people with disabilities.

Exploring and nurturing my spirituality within the framework of Christianity have provided the structure necessary for my spirit to soar. I have been able to find my calling through that structure. Although I believe God exists beyond it and beyond all words and worldly conceptions, I think it is difficult if not impossible for a human being to access the divine without following some spiritual path. When I engage in practices such as prayer or meditation, I benefit from the efforts of two thousand years of contemplatives and spiritual seekers who built on the efforts of one another to help define a path toward God. Practices such as maintaining balance in your life, ethical relationships, and moderation, which are found in Christianity as well as all major world religions, create a greater openness to the divine.

Many years ago I made a conscious choice to follow the Christian path. I don't consider my path any more legitimate than any other, but it was the path that spoke to me most profoundly. I believe that the religions of the world each point the way to the divine, which manifests itself differently to people in different cultures and times, through different prophets, speaking in a language they can understand. Anyone who seeks the divine with a sincere heart will find a path that leads, inexorably, closer to it.

As a UU Christian, I do not have the comfort and certainty that doctrine can provide. I sometimes experience confusion, periods of time when I don't know if my Christian beliefs are anything more than metaphor, and if they are not, what value they possess. The bad guys win and there is no meaning. Occasionally, I experience profound doubts about everything I believe and feel, as if I am in a terrifying free-fall. Sometimes God feels like an illusion. If I examine him too closely or fix my gaze for too long a time he disappears completely, and I am left with nothing.

Following my path keeps me from succumbing to despair. When I experience fear and uncertainty, I pray for guidance back to the path. Often these negative experiences are warning signs that I am out of balance or that my priorities have not been what they should be. Perhaps I am focusing on myself excessively or my motives are not pure. I remember things I have done wrong, take responsibility, apologize to God, and seek forgiveness. I surrender my fears and doubts to God and try to move forward. The advocate leads me on.

―◆―

CAROL STAMATAKIS *is a member of the Unitarian Universalist Church in Keene, New Hampshire. As an attorney, she focuses her efforts on environmental protection and government accountability.*

Why I Left
Unitarian Universalism

KAY ACHAR

Mine could have been the face on a Unitarian Universalist billboard: I went for my children and stayed for myself. But I only stayed about two years. Three months into my UU experience, unaware that I was opening the exit door, I asked my minister to recommend a book that would explain to me why people believe in God. Cautioning me that it was hardly a page-turner, he suggested William James's *Varieties of Religious Experience*. I devoured that five hundred-page book. And then I devoured it again. Not only did James explain to me why people believe in God, he enabled me to recognize God as the source of joy, gratitude, and confidence in the infinite moral significance of the universe, an intimate but nameless presence since my earliest memories.

The Anglican mystic and writer Evelyn Underhill writes, "The whole of religion, sanctity, and undeveloped spiritual life hinges on the incredible power to say 'Yes' or 'No' to God." After reading James, after a struggle with my humanist identity, I did say "Yes" to God. Immediately, questions arose: How can I know and serve God better? How and where can I offer God thanks and praise? I hungered for resources to help me implement the reality of God in my life. Finding little inspiration or help for growth and transformation in God in the UU setting and tradition, and in particular no guidance in the "unselfing" that is essential to sanctification, I turned to the writing of Christian mystics such as Julian of Norwich, John of the Cross, and Teresa of Avila, and teachers such as Tillich, Merton, Spong, and Borg.

About two years after my fall into theism, a friend directed me to an Episcopal church a half-mile from my home, which she had visited in response to a sign on the sidewalk near the front doors that beckoned, "This church is open for prayer all day and evening every day for people of all faiths or none." My friend said she thought I would like what I found there.

As a student of English literature, I had become intrigued by the tradition of John Donne, George Herbert, and T. S. Eliot. However, my understanding of the meanings of Holy Eucharist and the Nicene and Apostles' creeds was crude and literal, which might preclude feeling at home in an Episcopal church. Even so, I was thirsty enough to visit the well. I explained to the associate rector that although I could relate to the personality of God in the Holy Spirit, relating to divinity in the biblical figure of Jesus needed the aid of metaphor, that is, viewing him as the human face or the incarnate wisdom of God. I told her I was certain I couldn't avow the creeds in a literal sense. The priest replied that the church does not expect doctrinal uniformity and that no one at her church would require me to say or to do anything I wasn't comfortable saying or doing. Walking out of the church that day, a pamphlet on a table near the door caught my attention. The large white letters on the red cover stated, "This could be your church." And for now, at least, it is.

Today my faith is fully and satisfyingly expressed in a religion that is open to theological inquiry and debate, yet at the same time comprehensive, sacramental, liturgical, and sensual, with a deep tradition of prayer. Another pamphlet published by the Episcopal Church explains what my experience thus far affirms: What Anglicans believe can be found in the *Book of Common Prayer,* but it is only realized in the living of the faith.

I know that some people assume Christian avowal implies rejection of the truth or value of other religions. However, I don't believe that Christianity can lay claim to absolute value or absolute truth any more than Judaism, Islam, Buddhism, or Hinduism can. On the contrary, I believe that our religious thoughts and experiences have to do with matters that are ultimately mysterious, shaped by the doctrines and beliefs within which we explicate them. Therefore, I place a high value on an extremely rich shared language, liturgy, and literature because that currency of exchange facilitates both self-understanding and development and mutuality in community. Far from inhibiting my religious experience, then, worshiping, learning, and affiliating on the basis of a comprehensive and coherent shared body of thought and language makes growth and transformation in community more, rather than less, possible for me.

After I spent a couple of Sundays at the Episcopal church and participated in an eight-week spiritual formation course, my UU church seemed even less likely to offer the opportunities or means to help me address religious issues and questions. This was the Unitarian Universalism that was descended from the Boston Unitarianism of one hundred fifty years ago, which Henry Adams describes in his autobiography:

> They proclaimed as their merit that they insisted on no doctrine, but taught, or tried to teach, the means of leading a virtuous, useful, unselfish life, which they held to be sufficient for salvation. . . . That the most intelligent society, led by the most intelligent clergy . . . should have solved all the problems of the universe so thoroughly as to have quite ceased making itself anxious about past or future, and should have persuaded itself that all the problems which had convulsed human thought from earliest recorded time, were not worth discussing, seemed to him the most curious social phenomenon he had had to account for in a long life. The faculty of

turning away one's eyes as one approaches a chasm is not unusual, and Boston showed, under the lead of Mr. Webster, how successfully it could be done in politics; but in politics a certain number of men did at least protest. In religion and philosophy, no one protested.

Worship at my UU church had adapted to the secular world's fundamental fear of faith (that we can't be sure it's "right"). For example, the term *God* was always bracketed or qualified and there was never a time for corporate prayer. The sermons I heard at the church were consistently interesting and insightful, but they shed a lot more light on the minister's interests than on God's. Adult education classes took the 10,000-foot view, examined religion through the prism of universal myth without exploring what commitment or spirituality in any one religious tradition might entail, though events in the history of the Unitarian Universalist denomination were taught in some depth. UU community life had ceased to be relevant to my spiritual and religious needs and aspirations.

On the other hand, in the Episcopal parish I found opportunities, encouragement, and practical advice for both personal holiness and holy worldliness. Our worship centers on a liturgical calendar and includes prayer, interpretation of scripture, and the love feast of the Eucharist. Worship is intended as an opportunity to commune with God and to enlarge our understanding of God's nature and God's ways. Adult education is intended to help me deepen and clarify my relationship with God and to discern and develop my personal ministry in the world. I have joined a community that is diverse in race, ethnicity, age, relationship and family status, sexual orientation, income, educational attainment, and theological belief but nevertheless shares a living center, a core faith in God as all-inclusive love, from which our parish life springs.

―◆―

KAY ACHAR *is working on a doctoral dissertation on Christian sources in the thought and poetry of T. S. Eliot. She is a former member of Central Unitarian Church in Paramus, New Jersey. She now attends St. Mark's Episcopal Church in Teaneck, New Jersey.*

An Old Friend

ERIK WALKER WIKSTROM

Rev. L. B. Fisher, former editor of the denomination's newsletter, *The Leader,* was once asked what Universalism stood for. "We do not stand at all," he famously replied, "we move." The same can be said for Unitarian Universalists today. One of the principles around which we gather is a commitment to encouraging spiritual growth among our members and in our congregations as a whole. We are expected to grow and change and evolve in our understanding and our perspectives; ours is a religion of experiment and discovery.

The story of my own spiritual journey begins in the congregation of the First Presbyterian Church of Baldwin, New York (which may have the distinction of being the only Presbyterian church to produce two Unitarian Universalist ministers!). It moves quickly to Presbyterian and Methodist church camps. There I learned of a Christianity that was far more focused on building loving community than learning codified creeds. We took seriously the hymn that says, "They'll know we are Christians by our love," which, it's worth noting, does not say, "They'll know we are Christians by our dogmatic assertion of specific theological positions and our knowledge of proof texts." Such was the earliest stage of my spiritual journey.

Early on I felt a call to ministry. I was ordained as the youngest elder in the history of the Long Island Presbytery, and by my late teens I was working at those summer camps I'd attended. During the off-season, I traveled around New York and Connecticut as an itinerant freelance "clown minister," part of an informal network of mimes, clowns, puppeteers, magicians, and dancers using their theatrical skills in the service of religion. But I took my religion seriously. At home I was being exposed to transcendental meditation, Carlos Castenada, Joseph Campbell, Taoism, Wicca, and other spiritual expressions. You could say that the stage was set for my eventual conversion to Unitarian Universalism.

Despite—or perhaps because of—my deep involvement with Christian ministry from such a young age, I eventually reached a point at which the words and rituals no longer seemed to hold any meaning for me. Like so many others of my generation I found myself questioning and then rejecting the faith in which I'd been raised. I began a serious study of Zen Buddhism and dabbled in other traditions as well. Still feeling the call to ministry, I entered seminary, and by the time I was ordained thought of myself as a Zen Buddhist-Taoist-Wiccan-historically Christian-Unitarian Universalist.

This amalgam faith, with its amorphous and impersonal "Sacred Something," served me well until my mother died. I suddenly found myself experiencing a crisis of faith. My crisis was not that I had lost my faith but that I seemed to be finding it. I became aware of experiences—direct, personal experiences—that I could not fit into my hand-built theology. An impersonal force does not love, yet I felt loved. It does not call you into relationship, yet I felt such an invitation. And I remembered the sense of relationship I'd known during those summer camp days so long ago. None of this made sense to my well worked-out life philosophy, yet none of it could be denied either.

My exploratory Unitarian Universalism encouraged me to examine these experiences and to adapt my theology to them rather than try to force my experiences into some predefined theological box. In our tradition experience precedes theology; we are not told what we must believe, rather we are asked what we know to be true. I began to realize that, based on my own experiences, I still believed in a "Sacred Something." I cannot claim to fully know why, but this "Something" has consciousness and intent and is most definitely relational. I also found myself wanting to reconnect with the figure of Jesus of Nazareth, whom I once described in an Easter sermon as "an old friend I seem intent on forgetting." I wanted to renew the acquaintance.

Many have asked me how a Unitarian Universalist can be a Christian. The question is hard to comprehend because I honestly can't imagine any way of being a Christian without being a Unitarian Universalist. Our exploratory, experimental faith encourages us to question and examine everything and to accept as true only what we learn for ourselves. It offers us the freedom to seek widely among our human family's best attempts to answer life's questions, to draw upon the wisdom of all of the world's religions rather than limit ourselves to just one text or tradition. Only through this freedom could I have found the doors of the Christian tradition, which had once seemed so tightly closed, to be open and inviting once again.

From Buddhism, for instance, I learned that *Buddha* is simply a title conferred on someone who has had a spiritual awakening to the nature of reality and experienced a union with its underlying truth. Far from being reserved for the historic Buddha of 2,500 years ago, the sage Siddhartha, it is applied to anyone who has this awakening. Buddhist tradition holds that there were countless Buddhas before Siddhartha and that there are innumerable Buddhas to come. In the Zen tradition I studied, the goal of every practitioner is to realize her or his own innate Buddha nature. Rather than obsessing on a one-time-only incarnation, "Buddha-mind" is something that all of us should strive to manifest.

These teachings have given me new insight into the words of the apostle Paul, who writes about striving to have the mind of Christ grow in him until it is no longer he that lives but Christ that lives in him. (See, for instance, 1 Corinthians 2:16; Galatians 2:20.) Today I understand

Jesus to have been one who was so in touch with God as to be one with him. and those who saw him saw God. He was a window onto the sacred, a doorway to the holy. As the Gospels recall, he promised that all of the things he did his disciples would do as well. My study of Buddhism has helped me to understand Jesus as one who calls us to live out the full potential of our lives just as he did; to live out our heritage as beloved sons and daughters of the Divine Reality, to manifest the Christ in us as he did the Christ in him.

My study of Islam has helped me to more fully understand the spiritual journey as one of surrender. The world is what it is and no exercise of our own will can change it. As the ancient Roman Seneca said, "*Ducunt volentem lata, nolentem trahunt.*" (Him who will, the fates lead; him who won't, they drag.) We all face a fundamental choice: We can be smashed and dragged upon the rocks as we try to fight the river, or we can give up our own ego-centered willfulness and willingly allow ourselves to be carried along by the current. And since we are in our essence a part of the river that carries us, the flow of the current is our most authentic desire anyway. This is what Jesus meant by his insistence that we pray not for our own will but for an understanding of God's will for us. My encounters with Islam—the very name means "submission"—helped me see it.

Studying Judaism helped me to understand just how far modern Christianity has gotten from the religion Jesus experienced and expounded upon. Hinduism helped me to see that all of the goddesses and gods revered in the world's religions can be seen as different faces of one "Ultimate Reality." Religious humanism helped me to understand that science is not a contradiction of spiritual teaching but another revelation of the miraculous mystery in which we live and of which we are a part.

Many people have told me that they can understand how I see Jesus as my teacher and guide, but the idea of Jesus as a companion confuses them. How can I maintain that someone who died over two millennia ago can in any meaningful way be a present-day companion? Once again the wide study not only permitted but also actually encouraged by my Unitarian Universalist faith has provided an answer.

When I studied shamanic practice a question that arose again and again was whether or not the experiences in the shamanic world were "real" in the way that our experiences in the day-to-day world are. In other words, did we really talk with owls and run with wolves or were we just making it up? One teacher said that it really didn't matter. Even if it was only our imagination at work, even if our journeying was nothing more than a kind of lucid dreaming, there is universal agreement that we have much to learn from our dreams. On the other hand, he said that experienced shamanic practitioners can all tell stories about how they were convinced of the reality of their experiences. In time we would answer this question for ourselves.

Throughout the millennia that separate the death of Jesus and my life today countless women and men have claimed to experience the ongoing presence of that Galilean holy man; I can honestly say that I've experienced it myself. And who is to say that talking to Jesus is all that different than talking to a shaman's spirit guide? If my encounters with the living spirit of Jesus are nothing but my imagination at work, these dreams have much to teach me. And if, as my own lived experience convinces me, there is something more to it than that, who am I to deny it simply because it doesn't make sense to me? I don't understand electricity, either, but I don't have to if it works.

Over and over again my Unitarian Universalism has proved not an impediment to my Christian faith but a powerful aid. To be sure, the kind of Christian path I follow is not what many people mean by *Christianity,* but then I've never said I was a Pentecostal Christian or an Evangelical Christian—I am a Unitarian Universalist Christian. By this I mean that I am one who sees in the stories of Jesus the memories of a man whose union with the sacred was complete. He invited people into the mystery he called "God." I see in him the clearest example of the kind of life I wish to live, but I have no problem understanding that other people find clearer examples elsewhere. I find in the person of Jesus a present-day companion on my spiritual journey—challenging me, encouraging me, and supporting me as I pursue a pathless quest into the heart of the mystery itself.

ERIK WALKER WIKSTROM *is pastor of the First Universalist Church of Yarmouth, Maine, and the author of* Teacher, Guide, Companion: Rediscovering Jesus in the Secular World *and* Simply Pray: A Modern Spiritual Practice for Deepening Your Life.

I Am Convicted

VICTORIA WEINSTEIN

I can't remember a moment when Jesus first claimed me, but I remember the moment that Unitarian Universalism grabbed me for all time. I was about four years old and I was being dedicated along with my two siblings at our UU church in Westport, Connecticut. The minister, the kindly and very tall Ed Lane, crouched down to present me with a rose and spoke earnestly to me about my name and about the responsibilities of being a big sister to my infant brother. The congregation made murmuring "isn't this cute" noises, which irked me, but I nevertheless felt respected and cherished as an individual, by name. That feeling stayed with me through all my childhood years of sporadic attendance in UU congregations. Church was a place where I felt my questions were respected, and my concern for truth and integrity linked me to the community of elders. I liked the elders. They seemed smart and passionate and "with it" when they were at church, not fake-smiley and operating on autopilot, as I had seen at some of my friends' churches on Sunday mornings.

The trouble is, I never considered Unitarian Universalism a religion. I certainly didn't consider it *my* religion; it was just a place we went on Sundays. I suppose I thought of it along the lines of a political or social club. My parents liked it pretty well, and we kids liked it pretty well, but it made no real claims on us. Besides, everyone assumed I was Jewish so I thought I was too. Yet to this day I can count my appearances in a synagogue on one hand.

I came out of high school confused about religious identity and mourning the death of my father, my intense, existentialist/Jewish papa. Keenly motivated by grief and despair, I spent my late teens and early twenties searching for a spiritual home and experimenting with different theological orientations. I began my search in earnest at the Hillel House on the campus at Northwestern University, but was rejected by the rabbi (Reform, yet!) who told me that since my mother wasn't Jewish, neither was I. His opinion was amended by a Chabad-Lubavitcher Hasidic rebbe who kindly informed me, "If you're Jewish, that's between you and God." Blessed by this generous intimation of God's support of my religious freedom, I stopped trying to be theologically Jewish, left my studies with the rabbi, and continued my search. I discovered feminist spirituality and the Goddess and circled with the pagans for a while.

All the while, Jesus was hovering in the corner of my consciousness, installed there very early in life by a born-again babysitter, hokey old movies like *The Robe,* and *The Song of Bernadette,* a Russian Orthodox grandmother who used to surreptitiously sprinkle holy water on my sister and me as she tucked us into bed, and musicals like *Godspell* and *Jesus Christ Superstar.* A lot of my childhood friends had had Jesus hanging on a cross on their walls and around their necks, a grisly image that they regarded with comfortable complacency. It caused me to quietly jump out of my skin every time I encountered it. I intuited that this Jesus Christ person was either very connected to or synonymous with the spiritual presence I felt pulsing away at the heart of the world, but I had no idea how or why. Furthermore, both my parents and my church had insinuated that people who cared deeply about Jesus were, if not outright dumb, certainly weak, and that Christianity had offered no great contribution to the world that could possibly offset its legacy of prejudice, superstition, inquisitions, crusades, and ignorance. So I kept my distance.

When I returned to Unitarian Universalist congregational life in my twenties, it was more out of exhaustion and a lack of bright ideas than a true sense of belonging or calling. I flitted in and out of various UU churches and fellowships, remaining at the periphery and desperately wanting to be, in the language of the evangelical church, "convicted." I found the congregations I visited minimally friendly, minimally inspiring, and oriented almost entirely toward a 1960s generational experience of social justice activism whose rhetoric I found intolerant, self-righteous, and theologically empty.

But I was hungry for community and for spiritual growth, so I kept trying to attend church regularly, no matter how much it disappointed me. I tried to educate myself theologically in an intentional course of religious self-studies. I started with mythology and folklore, American Indian stories, the Upanishads, some of the Hebrew scriptures (again), the *Tao Te Ching* and little books with Buddha on the cover, and works by Huston Smith and Joseph Campbell. I found Jung and Elie Wiesel. I found Elizabeth Cady Stanton and John Donne. Finally, on the advice of a Wiccan friend who said she was tired of hearing me make insulting and ignorant remarks about Christians, I read Thomas Harpur's *For Christ's Sake,* which sent me straight back to the Gospels with a different perspective—a liberal religious perspective—and that stopped me cold.

I was convicted.

I spent about the next year or so feeling simultaneously embarrassed, thrilled, and frightened by my sense of calling to Christian spiritual life. I read and reread what I thought of as the "Jesus parts" of the Bible, and I kept my new passion a secret from everyone but my boyfriend, who patiently talked about Jesus with me far past his own interest level as a lapsed Lutheran. I had found my path, but I feared that it could not coexist with my own and my family's intellectual orientation, my affiliation with Unitarian Universalism, or my loyalty to my Jewish roots.

I remained a closeted Christian for several years, reading and thinking and teaching myself how to pray, discovering and respecting the troubled sibling relationship between Judaism and Christianity, and giving my heart and soul over to Christ as both man and spirit. I explored some Christian churches but was turned off by their literalism, their supercessionist treatment of Jewish religion, or their lack of commitment to social justice causes. I began to have more affection for Unitarian Universalism, now that I could see it within the larger context of American religious life.

But where was Jesus in our UU worship life? I had never once questioned his absence in my childhood church, but I now began to wonder. Since Jesus' radical inclusivity, love of humanity, and passion for justice was so harmonious with all the "good news" I was hearing in our congregations, why did our ministers and congregants so assiduously avoid the Gospels? I found it comical on some Sundays, depressing other Sundays, and consistently baffling. I could not understand why UUs would allow the perversions of the Religious Right to define the word *Christian* (or *religious,* for that matter), why they would concede religious language to the conservatives, and why they would go out of their way to construct a religion intentionally bereft of theology, rendering themselves a quasi-religion and many of their churches temples of denial and hypocrisy, where every spiritual path but the Christian path was considered valid and where all evidence of a Christian past was removed, revised, and painted over.

It took ten more years of committed Unitarian Universalist life for me to consider that perhaps my dear UUs were the most strangely faithful Christians of all. Having either intuitively or consciously embraced Jesus' gospel of love, service, and justice, they could not stand to affiliate with any so-called faithful who claimed to have received *their* inspiration for discrimination, exclusion, superstition, and damnation from the same source. The well, for too many UUs, had been irrevocably poisoned, and they would thereafter drink of the living waters from another source. Any other source, it seemed, but the Christian well. I felt called to abide with my religious community, to remain patient with my own sense of religious difference among them, and to pursue the ministry.

When I entered seminary I was still in the closet as a Christian, having read and found great spiritual kinship with Ralph Waldo Emerson but not yet with the Christian Unitarians of the classical era, whose nascent promise had been so damaged by the practically immediate rebellion of the Transcendentalists. That kinship with the "cloud of witnesses" would come later, after I had snuck into a meeting of the Unitarian Universalist Christian Fellowship in 1994, hoping to remain invisible on the sidelines, and been beckoned into the circle to take my first Communion with other Christians of my own stripe. There was no closet after that; there was a flood of learning and the shock and joy of discovery as I devoured thousands of pages written by our foremothers and forefathers who were religious liberals, Unitarian and Universalist Christians in theology and praxis, and whose heir I had been called to be.

Who is Jesus Christ to me? He is both a teacher of the Way, and the Way itself. For one who has always had a hard time grasping the concept of God, let alone developing a working definition of God, Jesus both points me toward a definition of God and then lives that definition. Jesus Christ is the freedom that laughs uproariously at the things of this world, while loving me dearly for being human enough to lust after them. He is my soul's safety from all harm. He is the avatar of aloneness, a compassionate and unsentimental narrator of the soul's exile on earth, and proof of the soul's triumphant homecoming at the end of the incarnational struggle. He is not afraid to put his hands anywhere to affect healing. He mourns, and weeps, and scolds, and invites. He is life more abundant and conqueror of the existential condition of fear.

"By their fruits ye shall know them," Jesus says in the Sermon on the Mount. There are indeed degenerate branches on the tree of Christian life, but this does not keep me from Christ. There are even disagreements among Unitarian Universalist Christians about the appropriateness of this or that perspective, practice, or teaching—debates that I regard mostly with affection, if occasionally with irritation. We have so much else to do. When I was baptized along with six others during a 1999 conference of the Unitarian Universalist Christian Fellowship, the event caused ecclesiastical consternation among some, but others expressed joy in welcoming more sisters and brothers to the body of Christ. Now we see in a glass, darkly. In the controversy surrounding my baptism I thought often and fondly of Rabbi Dov Klein's words, "If you're a Jew, that's between you and God." Thus it was at my baptism. It was between me and God, mediated by the love of friends and the presence of the Holy Spirit.

My daily Christian practice, although it changes frequently and is augmented by wisdom and practices from other traditions, consists mostly of clumsy efforts to love my God with all my heart, all my mind, all my soul, and all my strength, and to love my neighbor as myself. That's work enough for this lifetime.

I call myself a Christian because I am a disciple of Jesus Christ—not just Jesus-that-great guy-and-teacher-with-the-long-hair-and-sandals but Jesus the living avatar of the great God and Jesus the Christ of Easter morning. I have always said that I am a mystic at heart, and that if I had been born in pre-Christian times I would have been a devotee of the mystery religion of that time and place; perhaps the Eleusinian or Orphic rites. Christianity is the mystery religion of my time and place, and I am a devotee of it.

This last point, of course, distresses my rationalist Unitarian Universalist friends to no end, and I understand and accept that with affection and forbearance. But when we say that our living tradition draws from "direct experience of that transcending mystery and wonder, affirmed in all cultures, which moves us to a renewal of the spirit and an openness to the forces that create and uphold life," I think of that original community of disciples, who had a direct experience of the risen Christ that I revere and respect. It matters not at all whether I believe a dead man can be brought back to life or not, and although I used to research this question with some energy at the beginning of my Christian journey, today I have lost interest in exploring the scientific or historic whats, whens, and hows of the first Easter. Do I believe, then, in the resurrection? I believe that the original community of disciples had a direct experience of one who was truly dead, and who soon thereafter sent them out to love the world, to serve, to heal, and to overcome the forces of hatred and oppression.

And I am convicted.

―◦―

VICTORIA WEINSTEIN *is a Unitarian Universalist minister serving the First Parish Unitarian Church in Norwell, Massachusetts. She has also served congregations in Maryland and Pennsylvania.*

To Keep One's Soul

MARJORIE BOWENS-WHEATLEY

Upon her admission to a hospital some years ago, a woman was asked to state her religious affiliation. When she replied "Unitarian Universalist," the clerk reportedly looked up, smiled, and quietly typed "none" in the box.

It is not easy being a Unitarian Universalist. We are widely misunderstood in relation to the dominant culture, especially in the contemporary world of conservative religion and fundamentalism.

You may have seen these words on a bumper sticker: "God said it. I believe it. That settles it."

One-dimensional thinking such as this can lead to a desire never to discuss religion again. This is precisely the kind of thinking that led to the birth of liberal religion, to a creedless faith that does not impose a doctrine and does not oblige us to embrace a single truth.

I am among those who are in perpetual recovery from intolerance—indeed abuse—from a past religious experience.

At one level, you could say that the theological tenets my family sought to transmit to me simply "didn't take." My rational mind simply could not reconcile concepts like original sin, the virgin birth, and the resurrection. And so I lost faith completely, professing atheism for nearly a decade. But ultimately, after a crisis in my life, I had to find something to hold onto. So I took an inventory of all the religions that I had explored over the years and chose a path. The path I knew best, the one in which I felt most rooted—in spite of having been hurt by it—was Christianity.

After undergoing quite a painstaking healing process to "get over" my woundedness from the religion of my childhood and adolescence, I discovered that what I believed and tried to follow was the message of Jesus. It wasn't always smooth sailing. I struggled mightily with myself and with fellow Unitarian Universalists. I had to separate Christianity from the message of Jesus before I could begin to understand that there are as many forms (or perhaps nuances) of Christianity as there are of Unitarian Universalism.

When I became a Unitarian Universalist more than twenty years ago, I was proclaiming atheism and was delighted to learn that there was a spiritual community for people like me. But when I took the course "Building Your Own Theology" and other adult religious education courses with my minister, the late David Eaton, I began to realize that I had unnecessarily fallen into an "all or nothing" mentality—"thrown out the baby with the bath water." I had dismissed Christianity as irrelevant because

I experienced it as dogmatic and oppressive. Indeed, the particular form of Christianity that I grew up with *was* oppressive! Questioning was simply not permissible in an environment where biblical literalism prevailed. But in my lack of understanding about the diversity of Christianity, I had indulged in stereotyping; I assumed that if I knew one Christian, I knew them all.

I had to separate the history of the Christian Church from its theological tenets (many of which emerged not during Jesus' lifetime but centuries later). I also had to separate history and theology from the rules that governed the church and the widespread corruption I had witnessed in the church where I grew up.

Ultimately, I became a Unitarian Universalist who could explore religion in an atmosphere of freedom. But at one level, that freedom was theoretical and situational. Finding a congregation where I could be "out of the closet"—authentic in my Christianity—was difficult.

Eventually, I discovered that I was no longer a mere tourist exploring Christianity intellectually from the outside. I could finally claim it as my own, until Christian bashing among Unitarian Universalists raised its ugly head.

Today, Jesus remains a central figure of my religious identity. And yet I don't often call myself a Christian because there is no agreement on what the term *Christian* means, either within Unitarian Universalism or without. Even within Roman Catholicism and Protestantism, there are many interpretations of what it means to be a Christian.

There are conservative and liberal understandings of the Jesus story and Christian witness, and none of these has any exclusive claim on Jesus or those who seek to follow him.

In my Christian witness, no one's soul (or spiritual salvation) is dependent on a particular ritual, obligation, or statement of belief. There is no giant cop up in the sky dictating who will go up and who will go down. And yet I have been moved to tears by liturgical expressions of the story of Jesus and his work as a mystical teacher.

So reconciling the interpretations of my Christian past with a progressive Unitarian Universalism was not just a challenge for me; it took serious commitment and more than a decade to work through my issues and to embrace Jesus again.

I am profoundly moved by the message of Jesus as I understand it: liberation and freedom from oppression, love and compassion, service to others, and radical inclusiveness. His life and ministry continue to inspire me. Here was a man who challenged the laws, customs, and social expectations of his time. He affirmed the inherent worth and dignity of every person, even of the most marginalized in his day: women, prostitutes, the sick, and those who were scorned because they were not part of the dominant religious community. And he affirmed peace—not a passive peace but a peace in which we work proactively to bring about justice.

His values were so threatening to the powers-that-be that they executed him. Jesus' focal point of preaching and ministry was what he called "the kingdom of God," by which I believe he meant a state of being *in the here and now*. I prefer the term coined by Christian feminist Ada Maria Isasi-Dias, a Cuban theologian. She suggests that we consider Jesus' reference as a "kindom" of God, as an expression and recognition that we are all related, that we are brothers and sisters, called to create a new world through loving kindness, a world made new by the way we treat each other.

These universal values were also upheld by people like Mahatma Gandhi, Martin Luther King Jr., and Nelson Mandela, and we Unitarian Universalists claim them as well, as expressed in our seven Principles. And so I find it interesting when people ask: How can you be Unitarian Universalist and Christian at the same time? For me, there is no contradiction.

It's most accurate to say that I am a nominal Christian who has also found truth and wisdom in pre-Christian and mystical religions, earth-centered spiritualities, religious humanism, womanism, and other theologies of liberation. In addition, I have embraced the spiritual practice of Thai Chi and the wisdom of Buddhist philosophy. I am a Unitarian Universalist because I do not exclude *any* particular theology. As the spiritual says, there is "plenty good room" at the banquet table.

Most Unitarian Universalists are questioners, whether they are Christian, humanist, Buddhist, or pagan. Many of us chose this faith because it allows us the freedom to be ourselves, to be authentic, even with our doubts. It provides freedom from authoritarian hierarchy and creeds, and the possibility of truly keeping our souls without violating our own consciences.

If I have any advice for those struggling to discover their own truths, it is found in the ancient wisdom of a Sufi parable: If you want to move beyond a surface understanding of any religious tradition, you've got to dig a well—a well as deep as the self. You have to go into the depths of that tradition if you are to find the living water that awaits your thirst. Stated differently: Find a religious path—any path—and go as deeply as you can to understand and embrace it fully.

The path I have chosen is the path of Jesus, a path that is embraced by *some* Christians. Unitarian Universalism gave me the freedom to reclaim the message of Jesus—not in an oppressive way but in a way that is freeing, loving, caring, and compassionate. And Unitarian Universalism gives me the freedom to go beyond one path, to continue to explore and embrace different theologies, wherever truth is found.

In the Gospel of Luke, Jesus went into the temple, rolled out a scroll, and read these words from the prophet Isaiah:

> The Spirit of the Eternal is upon me, because he has ordained me and called me forth to bring good news to the poor. He has sent me to proclaim release to all who are in bondage, to recover sight to the blind, to

liberate all of the oppressed, and to proclaim Jubilee, the year of God's freedom and restoration.

These words are, perhaps, the best articulation recorded in the Gospels of the central focus of Jesus' ministry. I think of it as his mission statement: to bring good news to those who are most in need, to release those who live in bondage, and to bring freedom and healing to the world.

This is my mission statement as well, and the ministry to which I am called.

―◁○▷―

MARJORIE BOWENS-WHEATLEY *is associate minister of First Unitarian Universalist Church of San Diego. She has also served as adult programs director and field consultant for the Unitarian Universalist Association of Congregations and is currently a consultant for the JUUST Change Anti-Oppression Consultancy.*

In God's House
There Are Many Rooms

SCOTTY McLENNAN

I grew up as a conservative Presbyterian Christian in the Midwest. By the time I went to college, however, I identified myself as an atheist, largely because I couldn't understand how a just and loving God could allow all the horrible things that seem to go on in the world, especially the deaths of innocent newborns and children in natural disasters. These were even called "acts of God." So that was it for me.

When I arrived at college as an undergraduate in the mid-sixties, however, I encountered a dynamic university chaplain who was also a Presbyterian. He was offering something he called a "Seminar for Friendly Disbelievers." That seemed to describe me pretty well; I was a disbeliever but I wasn't really angry about it. I was a friendly, pleasant atheist. But at the same time, I couldn't help being utterly obsessed by the great existential questions about the meaning of life. Why are we here? Why do bad things happen to good people? What happens after we die? What happened before we were born? So I took the seminar.

The chaplain opened me up to a much more liberal view of Christianity as well as other world religions like Hinduism and Buddhism. By the end of my freshman year I'd signed up for a summer theology program in India, where I lived with a Hindu Brahmin priest and his family. Every morning I woke up to the sound of the names of 108 deities being chanted through the wall that connected my room to the *puja* room, or chapel, within the priest's home. Incense wafted around me and filled my lungs, and I felt spiritually transported even before I climbed out of my mosquito netting to start the day. I spent a lot of time reading and talking in India. I learned how to meditate with the priest, and we traveled to various Hindu temples and shrines. I heard a lot about the Hindu saint, Mahatma Gandhi, because my host was a non-violent activist who'd been involved in India's struggle for national liberation from the British.

One of the greatest surprises of my time in India was that the Hindu priest knew the Bible better than I did; he even kept a copy next to his bed. He'd also read the Islamic Qur'an from cover to cover and frequently recited passages. The priest seemed just as familiar with Buddhist scriptures. He spoke of many *avatars*, or incarnations of divinity, throughout history,—including Krishna, Buddha, and Jesus. As I sat cross-legged each day in my white cotton *dhoti* and *kurta*, I began to think, "Maybe this is the way to spiritual maturity: Be open to all religious traditions. Pick and choose what rings true for me in each." Yet the priest kept emphasizing getting on a path, following a discipline, becoming committed to a teacher and a set of teachings. "There are many well-marked paths up the spiritual mountain," he would say, "and they all reach the top, but you need to follow a path, and you can't be on more than one at a time."

At the end of the summer, I decided that I wanted to become a Hindu. The morning I told the priest, I was stunned by his response. "No, no!" he chided. "You've missed the point of everything I've taught you. You've grown up as a Christian and you know a lot about that path. It's the religion of your family and your culture. It's your ethics and your worldview. You know almost nothing of Hinduism. Go back and be the best Christian you can be."

I was upset. "But I don't believe Jesus was any more divine than Krishna or the Buddha," I pleaded. "And the Christians I grew up with would condemn you for knowing about Jesus and not accepting him as your only Lord and Savior." The priest's response was simple: "Then go back and find a way to be an open, non-exclusive Christian, following in Jesus' footsteps yourself but appreciating others' journeys on their own paths." The more I could learn about others' paths, he explained, the more I would progress along my own and deepen my understanding of it. Those words have remained my marching orders for life.

When I returned and told the college chaplain what I had learned, he seemed not to be understanding. Christianity, he reminded me, has historically insisted on the unique divinity of Jesus Christ. I explained that I took Jesus to be my own avatar, my personal lord and savior, but that I was convinced that other historical figures like Krishna and the Buddha had been equally filled with the spirit of God and were legitimately the personal lord and savior of many people. I also felt that continuing exposure to other traditions would energize my Christian faith. The chaplain reminded me of Jesus' claim in the Gospel of John that he was the way, the truth, and the life, and that no one could come to God except through him. I responded that in the same chapter of John, Jesus insists that in God's house there are many rooms. Surely some of those rooms housed Krishna, Buddha, and other avatars.

After many discussions along this line, this mainline Christian chaplain introduced me to Unitarian Universalism. "Go check out that denomination!" he nearly shouted at me one day in exasperation. "They seem to think like you and talk like you. That's the home for you." He called it a free tradition, appreciative of all the world's religions but without any dogma or doctrine binding its members. That meant there were people who put different adjectives before the words Unitarian Universalist—including Jewish, Christian, Buddhist, humanist, and agnostic. They were all welcome within the UU movement.

I started reading about Unitarian Universalism and going to a local church. I was delighted. I really did seem to have found my religion, although I wasn't sure it would sustain me beyond my questioning college days. Here I am, still at it, almost forty years later. Ironically, though, I've had some problems over the years as I've identified myself as a Christian within Unitarian Universalism. "Christianity!" some UUs have said to me. "That's exactly what we were trying to get as far away from as possible by becoming UUs. If it's Christianity you want, why don't you become something like a Presbyterian?" That response always takes me aback. "It's a long story," I say wearily, tempted to tell them of my Presbyterian chaplain's transformational words to a teenager about a tradition that appreciates all the world's religions and is free of dogma or doctrine binding its members. Instead, I usually just remind them that our Principles speak of Christian teachings as one of our sources and add that in God's house there are many rooms. I'm just trying to live as fully as I can in one of them, grateful to be part of a tradition that recognizes how big the house really is.

―◦―

SCOTTY MCLENNAN *has been a UU minister since 1975 and is the founder of the Unitarian Universalist Legal Ministry, based in a low-income neighborhood in Boston. He is also the dean for religious life at Stanford University, author of* Finding Your Religion: When the Faith You Grew Up Has Lost Its Meaning, *and co-author of* Church on Sunday, Work on Monday: The Challenge of Fusing Christian Values with Business Life.

A New Spirit

When the Unitarian Universalist Christian Fellowship held its first revival in February 1999 in New Orleans, it was clear that fresh winds were blowing through Unitarian Universalism. People were praying on their knees with their hands outstretched, or weeping or singing about Jesus with a passion not usually heard in a Unitarian Universalist church. Some were prayed over by the ancient practice of laying on of hands; others chose to be baptized. There was a new spirit among the small band of Christian Unitarian Universalists who attended that revival—and that spirit has continued to spread. What characterizes the difference?

Since 1945, the Unitarian Universalist Christian Fellowship has long been a faithful presence in Unitarian Universalism, publishing a respectable journal and maintaining a booth at General Assembly each year. What was unique about the 1999 revival was that it was primarily *devotional* in its stance. Unitarian Universalist Christians have long prided themselves on maintaining our rational and skeptical perspective on the Bible and various aspects of liberal Christianity. We have sought to analyze our faith and hold the Bible up to the cold light of truth and reason. But Unitarian Universalist Christians of today are also embracing a more devotional attitude toward worship, God, and our personal relationships with Jesus. Jesus has moved out of the safe confines of the discussion group and into the hearts and minds of those who wish to have a daily walk with God and with Jesus. In some Unitarian Universalist churches, this is readily embraced as part of the rich theological diversity that comprises our faith. Occasionally, fellow congregants will ask those who consider themselves Christians, "How can you be a Christian *and* a Unitarian Universalist?" Or, "You can be a Christian in any number of churches. Why don't you go there?"

Dave Dawson of the Thomas Jefferson Unitarian Universalist Church in Charlottesville, Virginia, responds in this way:

> I share a desire for the freedom to test the outer limits of my Christian faith. Within my church I am not told I am wrong, just looked at quizzically when I say I have a personal relationship with Jesus Christ. Occasionally I have had it suggested to me that I might be more comfortable somewhere else, but that is rare.

I also believe that the memory for tradition and history within the UUA is probably shorter by light years than it is in any other denomination. In two or three generations it is possible to pretend that our movement came from sources entirely outside of Christianity. Too often we as UU Christians are willing to not speak up for fear of offending newcomers, and we suffer as a movement. I believe we are far richer as a denomination when people see the rich diversity that welcomes Christians with a smile and a song.

Finally, I remain a UU Christian as a witness to those in mainline Christianity that, yes, universal salvation is alive and well, and it is a beautiful option for those people mired in shame-based churches. Over the past twenty years I have come to believe that salvation is indeed a process and not an event, and that God loves me more than I ever realized. I am incredibly grateful for the Christian leaders of Unitarianism and Universalism of the past and those of you who continue with me as UU Christians.

What is really the issue, then, behind the perceived marginalization of Christian Unitarian Universalists? Another way of framing the question is: How encompassing is Unitarian Universalism's theological umbrella? Is it truly large enough to shelter devotional Christians, rational Christians, devout atheists, humanists, agnostics, pagans, Buddhists, Jews, Muslims, and every theological orientation beyond and in-between? A first response may be "yes, of course!" because Unitarian Universalists pride themselves on theological diversity. However, tension arises when Unitarian Universalists gather for worship. How is our theological diversity represented? For UU Christians, the lack of engagement with the Bible or the teachings of Jesus means that a piece of our history and tradition is sorely missing. For the Unitarian Universalist atheist or humanist, the repeated use of scripture and references to God or Jesus are seen as embracing either the supernatural or a theological belief that they long ago rejected. What should we Universalists do? Create worship that is one-size-fits-all? Start theologically particular churches where God language is always used or never used? Or should we create opportunities for worship and discussion that represent our theological diversity?

Perhaps the best answer to these questions is "yes—all of the above." Some individuals have found that the culture and climate of their own Unitarian Universalist church are too dominant in one non-Christian theology to be comfortable. In response, some seek out a liberal Christian church in another denomination. More often, however, they will create a more Christo-centric Unitarian Universalist small group, where regular worship is a part of the experience. I long for the day when no Unitarian Universalist feels the need to migrate to another denomination to find spiritually satisfying community and worship. If Unitarian Universalists wish to practice the theological diversity that they preach, then all who seek a welcoming, liberal religious church would find their place in Unitarian Universalism. Christians, humanists, theists, atheists, agnostics, and others would share together not only their beliefs and how they came to hold those beliefs but how those beliefs inform their daily lives. In other words, how does one practice one's belief? How does one's theology *inform* one's decisions and behavior towards others? Does my Christian faith help me to turn the other cheek instead of taking offense? Does my humanist philosophy insist on seeing the best in humankind instead of the worst? Does my Buddhist practice make me more mindful of my interactions with others? Does my lifelong Unitarian Universalist faith compel me toward actions of personal sacrifice and social justice?

These are questions that reach beyond the scope of this book. The essays in this book point toward the diversity of experience, belief, and practice that exists within one small slice of Unitarian Universalism—the Christian experience. They raise a larger question about how those who identify as Christian Unitarian Universalists can be faithful, devoted, practicing, hyphenated Unitarian Universalists. It is my hope that as you put down this book, whether Christian or non-Christian, the stories you have read here of your fellow Unitarian Universalists have put both a smile on your face and a song in your heart.

Kathleen Rolenz

For Further Reading

Theology and the Bible

Altizer, Thomas J. J., and William Hamilton. *Radical Theology and the Death of God*. Indianapolis: Bobbs-Merrill, 1966.

Bawer, Bruce. *Stealing Jesus: How Fundamentalism Betrays Christianity*. New York: Three River Press, 1997.

Beach, George Kimmich. *Transforming Liberalism: The Theology of James Luther Adams*. Boston: Skinner House Books, 2004.

Borg, Marcus J. *The God We Never Knew: Beyond Dogmatic Religion to a More Authentic Contemporary Faith*. San Francisco: HarperSanFrancisco, 1997.

_____. *Meeting Jesus Again for the First Time: The Historical Jesus and the Heart of Contemporary Faith*. San Francisco: HarperSanFrancisco, 2001.

_____. *Reading the Bible Again for the First Time: Taking the Bible Seriously but Not Literally*. San Francisco: HarperSanFrancisco, 2001.

Brock, Rita Nakashimi, and Rebecca Parker. *Proverbs of Ashes: Violence, Redemptive Suffering, and the Search for What Saves Us.* Boston: Beacon Press, 2001.

Buehrens, John A. *Understanding the Bible: An Introduction for Skeptics, Seekers, and Religious Liberals.* Boston: Beacon Press, 2003.

Bumbaugh, David. *The Education of God.* London: Rising Press, 1994.

Gomes, Peter. *The Good Book: Reading the Bible with Mind and Heart.* New York: HarperCollins, 1996.

Harpur, Thomas. *For Christ's Sake.* Boston: Beacon Press, 1987.

Jesus Seminar. *The Gospel of Jesus: According to the Jesus Seminar.* Edited by Robert Walter Funk. Santa Rosa, CA: Polebridge Press, 1999.

Mitchell, Stephen. *The Gospel According to Jesus.* New York: HarperCollins, 1991.

Muir, Fredric. *Heretics' Faith: Vocabulary for Religious Liberals.* Self-published, 2001.

Norris, Kathleen. *Amazing Grace: A Vocabulary of Faith.* New York: Riverhead Books, 1998.

Rasor, Paul. *Faith Without Certainty: Liberal Theology in the 21st Century.* Boston: Skinner House Books, 2005.

Spong, John Shelby. *Rescuing the Bible from Fundamentalism: A Bishop Rethinks the Meaning of Scripture.* San Francisco: HarperSanFrancisco, 1991.

_____. *The Sins of Scripture: Exposing the Bible's Texts of Hate to Reveal the God of Love.* San Francisco: HarperSanFrancisco, 2005.

_____. *Why Christianity Must Change or Die: A Bishop Speaks to Believers in Exile.* San Francisco: HarperSanFrancisco, 1998.

Wright, Conrad, ed. *Three Prophets of Religious Liberalism: Channing, Emerson, Parker.* Boston: Skinner House Books, 1996.

History and Culture

Anderson, Leith. *Jesus: An Intimate Portrait of the Man, His Land, and His People.* Minneapolis: Bethany House, 2005.

Maurin, Peter. *Easy Essays.* Quincy, Ill.: Franciscan Herald Press, 1977.

Niebuhr, H. Richard. *Christ and Culture.* New York: HarperPerennial, 1956.

Prothero, Stephen. *American Jesus: How the Son of God Became a National Icon.* New York: Farrar, Straus and Giroux, 2003.

Schweitzer, Albert. *The Quest of the Historical Jesus*, translated by W. Montgomery. New York: Macmillan, 1968.

_____. *Christianity and the Religions of the World*, translated by J. Powers. London: George Allen, and Unwin, 1923.

Schonfield, Hugh J. *The Passover Plot: A New Interpretation of the Life and Death of Jesus*. New York: Bantam Books, 1965.

Spirituality and Prayer

Davies, A. Powell. *Without Apology: Collected Meditations on Liberal Religion*. Boston: Skinner House Books, 1998.

Wikstrom, Erik Walker. *Simply Pray: A Modern Spiritual Practice to Deepen Your Life*. Boston: Skinner House Books, 2005.

_____. *Teacher, Guide, Companion; Rediscovering Jesus in a Secular World*. Boston: Skinner House Books, 2003.